Let's get reading...

The Kindle goes from strength to strength. With every new release, Amazon proves once again why its digital ebook device is the most talked about reader of all.

It's far from the only option. There are plenty of rivals from equally high-profile players, each backed up by extensive stores of books just waiting for you to download – some for slightly less than their regular printed price; many for free.

It's the Kindle, though, that most people think of first when they picture an ebook, and the line's latest updates have done nothing to damage that well earned reputation.

There's never been a better time to buy one, either. Publishers have cottoned on to the fact that they can't afford not to produce digital versions of their books, which means you can make some real savings by going paper-free. Amazon itself is getting in on the act, publishing a select range of ebooks of its own, and it's increasing the abilities and features of its ereaders all the time. They can now subscribe to blogs, download magazines and play music, as well as rendering plain old text and graphics on screen.

The line is now split in two, with the traditional e-ink-based readers receiving modest updates, making them slightly smaller, cheaper and faster. They'll appeal to the avid bookworm, who will enjoy the look of the reflective screen that most closely resembles the traditional printed page.

But they're not your only choice. The other half of the Kindle line comprises the Kindle Fire and Kindle Fire HD, two exciting low-cost tablet devices, that as well as being able to access the whole of Amazon's regular library of downloadable books can also play music and movies, surf the web, send and receive emails, and install third-party software.

In this guide, we'll help you identify the Kindle that best suits your needs and set it up once you get it home. We'll show you how to get online, download books and other content, and start enjoying the exciting world of reading without paper.

— *Nik Rawlinson*

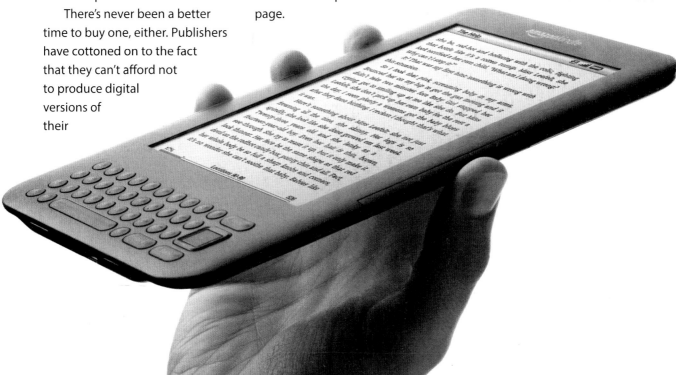

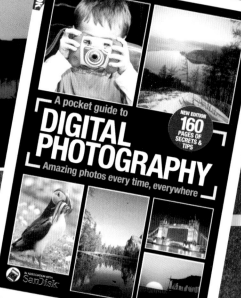

Ultimate Guide to Kindle

WRITTEN BY Nik Rawlinson

MANAGEMENT
MagBook Publisher Dharmesh Mistry
Digital Production Manager Nicky Baker
Operations Director Robin Ryan
Managing Director of Advertising Julian Lloyd-Evans
Newstrade Director David Barker
Commercial & Retail Director Martin Belson
Chief Operating Officer Brett Reynolds
Group Finance Director Ian Leggett
Chief Executive James Tye
Chairman Felix Dennis

MAGBOOK™

LICENSING & SYNDICATION
To license this product, please contact Carlotta Serantoni on +44 (0) 20 7907 6550 or email carlotta_serantoni@dennis.co.uk. To syndicate content from this product please contact Anj Dosaj Halai on +44 (0) 20 7907 6132 or email anj_dosaj-halai@dennis.co.uk.

Contents

Buying your first Kindle

Reading with your Kindle

ONE

t I was being followed long before I saw
y pursuer. I felt it by some instinct that
ad been sharpened by experience; a
the air, a presence whose movements
hadowed my own. Someone was
ne and had been for several days: from
s of alleyways, from behind pillars or
d the crowds of people, carts and
at thronged the narrow streets of
out among the river traffic. At times I
d eyes on me in the privacy of my room
ry Court, though that was surely
and could only have been the tricks of
a.
e twenty-third day of July, 1584, and I
ng to deliver my new book to my printer
eft London for the rest of the summer. A
hip from Portugal had recently docked

kindle

Kindle Hacks

Kindle Fire

Kindle Fixer

Buying your first Kindle

Choosing the right Kindle for your needs

£69 to £199

Buying a Kindle is your first step into an exciting new world of digital reading. You may not believe it right now, but many people who switch from pages to pixels soon can't go back.

There's no need to fumble with a bookmark, no chunky volume to weigh down your bag, and the convenience of being able to carry a whole library and buy new books wherever you go.

Over the years, Amazon has released a series of Kindles, each one lighter and more powerful than its predecessors. They're keenly priced and offer similar features, and while this may mean that whichever one you buy it'll do just as good a job of managing and displaying your books as any of the others, it also introduces a degree of confusion.

On this spread, we'll run through the various features of the four main Kindles to help you get to grips with their differences and identify which one would likely be your perfect reading companion. It's important to get this right, as while you might discard a book when you've finished it, you won't do the same with your Kindle – it's your reading companion for life.

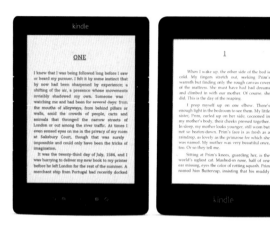

	Kindle	Kindle Paperwhite
Screen size	6in	6in
Display technology	e-ink	Paperwhite e-ink
Resolution	167 pixels per inch	212 pixels per inch
Audio	None	Stereo speakers
Connectivity	USB / Wifi	USB / Wifi / 3G
Storage	2GB	2GB
Dimensions	16.5 x 11.4 x 0.87cm	16.9 x 11.7 x 0.91cm
Weight	170g	213 - 222g
Battery life	Up to 1 month	2 months
Interface	Multi-way controller plus side buttons	Touch-sensitive screen
Price	£69	£109 / £169

At-a-glance buyers' guide. Turn the page for full reviews.

Kindle Keyboard **Kindle Fire** **Kindle Fire HD**

Kindle Keyboard	Kindle Fire	Kindle Fire HD	
6in	7in	7in	**Screen size**
e-ink	Colour LCD	Colour LCD	**Display technology**
167 pixels per inch	1024 x 600 pixels	1280 x 800 pixels	**Resolution**
Stereo speakers	Stereo speakers	Stereo speakers with Dolby processing	**Audio**
USB / Wifi / 3G	USB / Wifi	USB / Wifi	**Connectivity**
4GB	8GB	16GB or 32GB	**Storage**
19 x 12.3 x 0.85cm	18.9 x 12 x 1.15cm	19.3 x 13.7 x 1.03cm	**Dimensions**
274g	400g	395g	**Weight**
2 months	Almost 9 hours continuous use	Over 11 hours continuous use	**Battery life**
Full keyboard plus multi-way controller and side buttons	2-point multitouch screen	10-point multitouch screen	**Interface**
£149	£129	£159 / £199	**Price**

Kindle

£69

The entry-level Kindle is the cheapest e-reader Amazon has ever produced, and it gets better with every update.

It's easy to see how the company has managed to make this model of Kindle so affordable: it's seriously stripped down when compared to its siblings, with neither a hardware keyboard nor a touch-sensitive display on offer. There's no 3G option here, so if you don't have a wireless network at home you'll have to either buy your books wirelessly on a public network or at work, or download them to your computer and transfer them using the bundled USB cable. There's also no plug in the box, so if you don't want to

KINDLE QUICK FACTS	
Screen size	6in
Display technology	e-ink
Resolution	167 pixels per inch
Audio	None
Connectivity	Wifi / USB
Internal storage	2GB
Dimensions	16.5 x 11.4 x 0.87cm
Weight	170g
Battery life	Up to 1 month
Interface	Multi-way controller plus side buttons

buy one as an optional extra you'll have to charge your device by plugging it into a spare USB port on your computer.

American shoppers can cut the cost of buying this most basic of all Kindles still further by opting

for the version with what Amazon calls 'special offers'. This translates to adverts, which are displayed on the home screen and in place of the images that are shown when the Kindle is switched off. The offers don't appear within the pages of your books, so they won't interrupt your reading, and they are genuinely useful in many cases, with past offers including Kindle books for $1 or savings of up to $500 on high definition televisions. These offers are not currently available outside of the US, where shoppers have to pay the full price for their device.

It has a 6in e-ink screen, which is great in bright light but, as is the case with a physical printed book, less effective in dimmer

surroundings. Both Amazon and several third-party manufacturers therefore sell covers with built-in lights that make it much easier to read. The latest generation of Kindles have a very fast screen refresh rate – 15% faster than their predecessors – which largely overcomes the problem of the flash you see when turning a page.

Amazon has also tuned the on-screen fonts used in the latest generation Kindles to give them smoother edges and a darker, more impactful appearance, which should make for a more pleasant reading experience – particularly if you use your Kindle for extended periods. If that sounds like you then you'll also be pleased with how light and thin it is; a pencil is thicker than this diminutive device.

Although this model has the lowest storage capacity of any Kindle in the range, it will nonetheless allow you to carry 1,400 books at any one time, which should be more than enough for even the longest holiday or career break. It also has the lowest-powered battery, yet can keep running for a month on a single charge so long as you read for around half an hour a day and keep the wireless networking

features switched off, the only effect of which would be that your current page position and bookmarks won't be synced.

As with the other Kindles, it can download books in less than 60 seconds and they'll be backed up in Amazon's cloud system so you can download your purchases again in the future whenever you choose. It has adjustable text sizes and three fonts to choose from and can share highlights and notes online, so long as you're prepared to use the four-way controller to hunt about the on-screen keyboard when tapping out your jottings. It doesn't take long to get used to working this way, and you'll soon forget that you don't have a proper physical keyboard to work with.

Kindle Paperwhite

£109 to £169

One step up from the basic Kindle is the Kindle Paperwhite. At first, it appears to be very similar to the entry-level device, but look closer and you'll see that it's dropped the buttons that appear on the panel at the bottom of its front surface, as well as the forwards and backwards page-turning buttons that sit one above the other on either side of the body. To use it, you instead interact directly with the screen, as you would with a regular tablet device.

This will appeal to many users as it's a way of working that we are all now becoming used to thanks to the proliferation of smartphones that rely on us swiping and tapping the screen

to control their various functions. Interacting directly with the pages is also much more similar to the way that we handle traditionally printed books, so it may be just enough to tempt the Kindle doubters into making the switch.

Buttons aside, the Paperwhite differs in one very important way to the basic Kindle in that the screen is backlit, so you can read it in the dark – perfect if you share a bed with someone who tends to go to sleep before you.

This illumination is implemented in a very different way to the light that runs behind the screen on the Kindle Fire, which instead uses an LCD display. The Paperwhite, which still uses e-ink in front of the illuminated panel, should prove to be more relaxing when read for extended periods.

The Paperwhite has sufficient internal capacity to hold around 1100 books, as 1.25GB of the installed 2GB remains free for use

KINDLE PAPERWHITE QUICK FACTS

Screen size	6in
Display technology	e-ink
Resolution	212 pixels per inch
Audio	Built in stereo speakers
Connectivity	Wifi / USB /3G
Internal storage	2GB
Dimensions	16.9 x 11.7 x 0.91cm
Weight	213 – 222g
Battery life	2 months
Interface	Touch-sensitive screen

e-ink vs LCD

You might wonder why you'd buy an e-ink Kindle when you could bag yourself a full-colour Kindle Fire. The Fire has its attractions – particularly the ability to install fully-fledged Android apps – but e-ink has many benefits if you'll spend more of your time reading than anything else. For starters, the experience is far more like reading paper, and it has a wider viewing angle, which means you may find it more comfortable to hold an e-ink Kindle than an LCD one as you don't have to worry about shifting colours and reflections. There is also some evidence to suggest that e-ink doesn't affect your sleep patterns the way that LCD can in some people, which is good news for anyone who enjoys reading their Kindle last thing at night to help them nod off.

once the operating system has been accounted for. It's a greyscale device, capable of differentiating between 16 different levels of grey, which might not sound like much, but when you take into account the fact that it dithers each of these tones in a pattern to imitate a far broader spectrum it's actually very effective.

The battery is more powerful than the one found in the plain Kindle, and in regular use, which Amazon counts as being around half an hour of reading a day with the wireless networking features turned off, you can expect to get around two months' use from a single charge.

Again, this Kindle isn't shipped with a power adaptor so you'll have to either charge it by plugging it into an available USB port on your computer or buy an optional adaptor add-on. Charging through a USB port takes around four hours to complete. Using the optional charger is quicker.

The arrival of the Paperwhite marks the return of 3G to Amazon's touch-based e-ink Kindle line-up (a wifi only version is available), which previously had been confined to the Kindle Keyboard. That means you can download books on the move and access content through your free account on Amazon's online Cloud Drive.

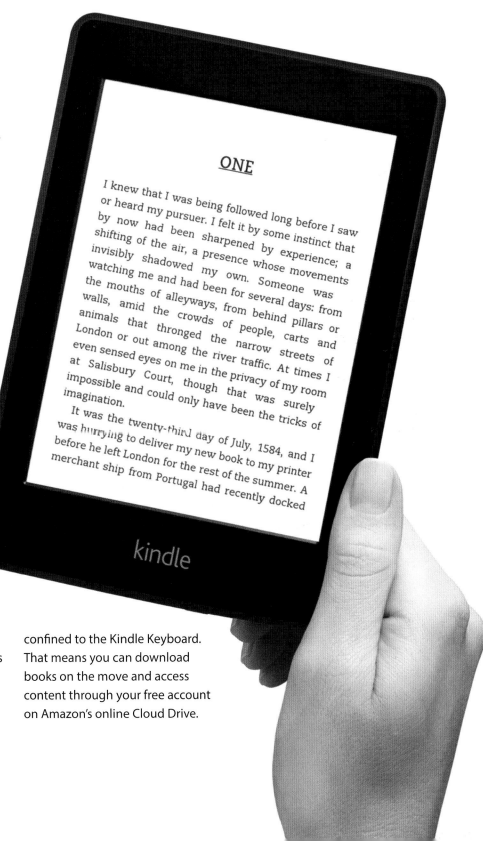

Kindle Keyboard

£149

The **headline product** from the Kindle line-up of two generations ago lives on as part of the ever growing family. The Kindle Keyboard was previously known as the plain old Kindle 3, first appearing in 2010 and marking a significant shrinking down in physical size of Amazon's hardware e-reading devices.

Despite shipping in a larger case it has the same 6in e-ink screen as the Kindle and Kindle Paperwhite, although without the touch-sensitive layer of the latter. It extends the Kindle feature set to offer 3G networking in addition to regular wireless Ethernet. That means that, so long as you buy the 3G edition, this is the only Kindle

KINDLE KEYBOARD QUICK FACTS	
Screen size	6in
Display technology	e-ink
Resolution	167 pixels per inch
Audio	Built in stereo speakers
Connectivity	Wifi / 3G / USB
Internal storage	4GB
Dimensions	19 x 12.3 x 0.85cm
Weight	274g
Battery life	2 months
Interface	Full keyboard plus side buttons

on sale that lets you buy books and browse the web remotely without being connected to your own wifi network.

It beats the Paperwhite's storage capacity of 2GB, and so has more than twice the amount

of free space left over once the operating system has been accounted for than the plain entry-level Kindle does. That means you can carry a larger number of books at any one time – up from 1,400 to a massive 3,000, which should be enough for even the most vociferous reader on the longest sabbatical.

The biggest and most noticeable difference, though, between this any other Kindle is the fact that this is the only one with a physical keyboard. Its keys may yet be fairly small, but they make a significant difference to the useability of the device, particularly when searching the online store and tapping out short notes related to the content of

your current book that you want to tweet, post to Facebook or remember to reference later.

Look closely and you'll also notice that the page turning buttons, which sit on either side of the casing, are also larger on the Kindle Keyboard than they are on the regular, plain Kindle. This makes them easier to press, and some users will find this a physically more comfortable and convenient Kindle to hold for extended periods.

The Kindle Keyboard ships in a larger box to make room for a bundled power adaptor. This is a significant boon for anyone who doesn't want to have to resort to charging their device by plugging it into a free USB port on their computer, and anyone who thinks they might need to charge it while they're away from home, as it means you won't have to splash out extra on the optional charger that Amazon sells as an add-on for the Kindle and Kindle Paperwhite.

A single charge should see you through two months of reading if you keep the networking features turned off and read for an average of two hours a day. The 3G connection has no ongoing fees, but keeping this turned on will drain the battery more quickly, so it's better not to use this for synchronisation.

It may not be the latest, greatest addition to the Kindle family, but for our money the Kindle Keyboard remains perhaps the best Kindle ever made, and for that reason we're very happy to see it live on in this latest iteration. We would, however, have liked to see Amazon keep the wifi-only version around for those readers who don't envisage needing to buy books while away from home, and perhaps offering that as a separate option at a cheaper price. However, we can see why it didn't: £149 is a bargain already. Dropping it any further might dent the appeal of the Kindle and Kindle Paperwhite.

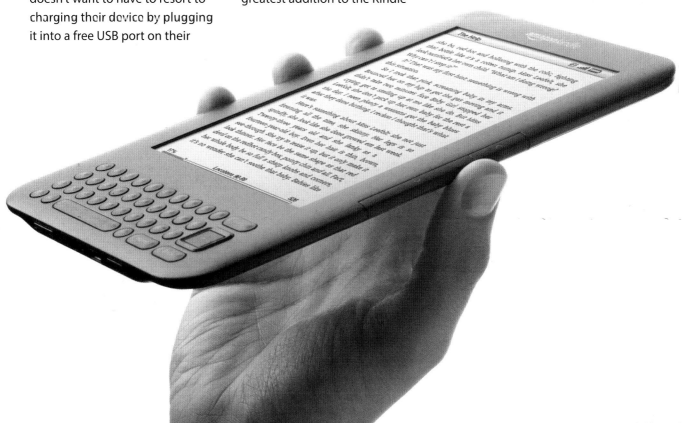

Kindle Fire

£129

The Fire was once the odd one out in the Kindle family, as it's actually a full-blown tablet rather than a simple e-reading device. However, this latest revision has been joined by another LCD-based tablet: the more powerful Kindle Fire HD.

Fire jettisons the other Kindles' 6in greyscale e-ink screens in favour of a 7in, 1024 x 600 resolution, full colour display which, like the Kindle Paperwhite, is fully touch-sensitive, allowing for far greater control.

It also does away with the simplistic operating system that underpins the rest of the Kindle family, swapping it out for a more capable Amazon-tuned variant of Android, the Google-originated OS

KINDLE FIRE QUICK FACTS	
Screen size	..7in
Display technology	LCD
Resolution	..1024 x 600 pixel display
Audio.	.. Built in stereo speakers
Connectivity	Wifi / USB
Internal storage	8GB
Dimensions	18.9 x 12 x 1.15cm
Weight	400g
Battery life	Almost 9 hours continuous use
Interface..	2-point multitouch

that runs many smartphones and tablet computers. This means it can access a whole world of third-party applications, downloaded from the Amazon Appstore.

Under the hood there's a powerful 1.2GHz dual-core

processor and 8GB of internal memory. Using Amazon's own calculations, that's enough to store 80 applications alongside 800 songs, 10 full-length feature films or 8,000 books.

Content is downloaded wirelessly using the built-in wifi networking features, but it lacks Bluetooth support, which would allow you to add an external keyboard or wireless headset, and the 3G connectivity option featured on the Kindle Keyboard, so when you're away from your home or office network – or a public network – you won't be able to browse the web or send emails.

Amazon includes a power adaptor in the box. However, because of the screen technology

and underlying hardware a single charge won't last you as long on the Fire as it would on the e-ink-based Kindles. This latest revision of the entry-level Fire can run for around nine hours on a single charge, which is an improvement of one hour over its predecessor.

Kindle Fire owners have access to 10,000 movies and TV shows, an unrivalled online book store, including 5,000 free books, and 17 million songs. It also gives access to the Amazon Cloud service, which is an online home for all of your content, allowing you to store documents and files, and re-download any of the content you have bought in the past

without paying for any of it a second time around.

All of this points to the fact that Amazon sees the Kindle Fire more as a device for consuming all of the different kinds of content that it sells through its online store, which isn't something you can say about the greyscale Kindles. They can't handle movies at all, don't all support audio, and aren't built to interact fully with your social networks or have their features extended with newly downloaded apps.

The Fire is really a Kindle in name only. If all you want to do is read books, turn back a page or two and check out the Kindle, Kindle Touch or Kindle Keyboard. If you want to watch movies and work on the move, though, turn ahead to the Kindle Fire HD, too, before making your final decision on which to buy.

Kindle Fire HD

from £159

After the success of the original Kindle Fire, which was only released in the US, it was only natural that Amazon should want to follow it up with a more impressive device that it would sell in more territories. That device is the Kindle Fire HD.

There are several different versions of the Fire HD. Outside of the US it comes in only one size, with a 7in screen sporting an impressive resolution of 1280 x 800 pixels. However, under the hood you'll find a choice of capacities, with integrated flash memory running to either 16GB (for £159) or 32GB (for £199). Of this, there's 12.6GB left free on the 16GB device for you to fill with

your own choice of applications, books and live media. On the 32GB, there's 26.8GB free. If you can afford it, and you'd a rapacious consumer of music and movies, it probably makes sense to buy the more capacious device as

you're getting identical specs in every other respect, but doubling the storage capacity for a very reasonable £40.

If most of what you'll be doing involves browsing the web and dealing with your email, however, the lower-capacity device will probably suit you fine, but bear in mind that you'll also have less space for applications that you download from the Amazon Appstore.

The Kindle Fire HD is slightly larger than the regular 7in Kindle Fire, and it weighs more, too, but much of this additional bulk is more than offset by the increased battery life of up to 11 hours per charge and the more able multitouch screen, which is

KINDLE FIRE HD QUICK FACTS	
Screen size	..7in
Display technology	LCD
Resolution	..1280 x 800 pixel display
Audio.	. Built in stereo speakers with Dolby output
Connectivity	Wifi / USB
Internal storage	16GB or 32GB, depending on model
Dimensions	.. 19.3 x 13.7 x 1.3cm
Weight	395g
Battery life	.Over 11 hours on wifi
Interface	.. 10-point multitouch

sensitive to 10 points, rather than the two point sensitivity on the regular Kindle Fire.

Amazon is rightly making much of the fact that the Kindle Fire HD has two powerful speakers built in with exclusive Dolby Digital audio, which will make the Fire HD the best choice of all of Amazon's various portable offerings for enjoying movie and TV content – along with singles and albums – downloaded from the store and stored in your Amazon Cloud account.

In the United States, there are two other Kindle Fire HD models to choose from. As well as the two discussed here, Amazon has produced the Kindle Fire HD 8.9". As its name suggests, it has a screen that's almost two inches larger from corner to corner, with a higher resolution to match: 1900 x 1200. That makes several desktop monitors. Behind it you'll also find higher storage capacities, with a choice of either 32GB or 64GB. It also offers a version with built-in cell network connectivity so you can be productive on the move, without an active wifi connection.

There's no word on when (or even if) these will be available outside of the US, but it's certainly not beyond the realms of possibility, as Amazon, like several other manufacturers, seeks to satisfy demand in its home market first and only then starts selling the same products overseas.

Kindle competitors

Amazon's Kindle range may well be the best-known line-up of e-reading devices available, but they're far from the only ones. Neither was the first Kindle the earliest e-reader on sale: Amazon's readers have simply carved themselves a niche as some of the best supported and widest used readers worldwide.

Choosing an e-reader is about far more than just picking the best hardware for your needs. As each one is usually tied into a dedicated online store you should also consider the price of the books on sale and the size of the range on offer. There is no point buying into a poorly-supported platform, after all.

Each of the e-readers in the line-up here is well supported by an extensive online library, and they also use the widely adopted ePub format for their books, which means it's possible to buy books from rival stores and load them onto each one. That's less often the case with the Kindle, which uses a variation on Mobipocket as its native format and, to date, isn't compatible with ePub.

There is an added advantage to using ePub, which is that more libraries support the format. At the time of writing, library lending is only compatible with the Kindle in the United States, meaning that UK readers who want to borrow books to reduce the cost will have to opt for one of these alternatives.

Each of these devices is available in regular retail stores, making it easy to buy books from traditional high street retailers' online shops, giving them a library to rival that offered by Amazon.

Sony Reader

The Sony Reader can store up to 1,300 books or documents in its internal memory and has a MicroSD card slot for expanding its capacity, allowing you to travel with an unlimited number of books at your disposal.

The screen is 6in diagonally from corner and has a resolution of 800 x 600 pixels. It comes in three colours – black, red and white – with a 1 month battery life, which matches the entry-level Kindle.

The screen is touch-sensitive; you swipe to turn from one page to the next, and pinch or unpinch, as you would on the iPad, to zoom out and in. As well as the regular British and American English dictionaries it has ten built-in translation dictionaries.

Price £119
Link www.sony.co.uk/reader

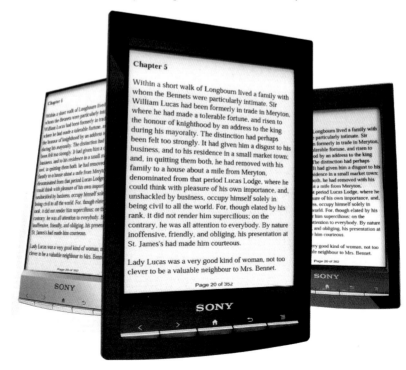

Kobo readers

Kobo makes an enormous range of e-readers, from the diminutive Mini, with its pocket-friendly 5in screen, to the more conventional Kobo Touch and backlit Kobo Glo.

All are tied in to the Kobo store, which offers a choice of nearly 3m books, magazines and newspapers, which you can buy direct from the device. Every reader has a built-in dictionary and lets you choose from a range of font faces and sizes to customise your reading experience.

Although you can buy them online from a variety of sources, Kobo has done a deal with WHSmith to sell them on the high street, giving you the chance to try before you buy.

Price From £59
Link kobo.com

Nook Simple Touch and Simple Touch GlowLight

The Simple Touch has a 6in e-ink based touch screen, like the Kobo Touch and Kindle Paperwhite. It has a built-in dictionary and a choice of fonts in a range of sizes.

The battery lasts for over two months on a single charge, and the Nook store has over 2.5 million ebooks, magazines and newspapers to download. They're downloaded using the built-in wifi, and personalised recommendations appear on the home screen to help you choose your next book.

The GlowLight builds on the features of the Simple Touch by adding a light behind the screen that lets you read in the dark the way you would on an LCD.

Price £79 / £159
Link nook.co.uk

How to register your new Kindle

If you buy your Kindle directly from Amazon it will already be set up, registered to your account and ready for use.

If you bought it from a supermarket, electrical store or other high street shop, however, it won't have any of your details to hand and you'll have to add them yourself by stepping through the easy registration process.

Registering your Kindle isn't simply a means of giving your data to Amazon so that it can send you offers and emails, as you may consider to be the case when you register software or an electrical appliance. Instead, registration is an essential part of setting up your device and getting it ready to use. It ties it to your Amazon account so that all of your payment details and gift vouchers will be available to use when you purchase books directly through the device.

The Kindle uses Amazon's one-click purchase system, whereby clicking the Buy Now button on a book's listing page immediately buys and downloads the title (although if you bought it by accident, so long as you haven't started reading it you can easily cancel the download, remove the book from your device and receive a refund).

To facilitate registration, every Kindle is assigned a unique serial number. Press the menu button and select Settings and you'll find yours at the bottom of the screen (press *Settings* | *More* | *Device* to find it on Kindle Fire). If you have a Kindle Keyboard you can find it by holding shift and alt and pressing full stop, or by looking at the bottom of the menus.

The shortcut pulls up a blank screen with two barcodes and your unique serial number (*grab 1, below*). Keep this secret and don't share it with friends, but make a note of it for use in the next step.

Now log in to your Amazon account using a regular browser and click *Kindle* | *Manage Your Kindle* | *Register a Kindle* (you'll find the last link in the left-hand menu box) to start the process of tying your new Kindle to your existing Amazon account.

Type the serial number you noted from your Kindle menus into the Serial Number box and click *Register*. This ties your Kindle to your account and authorises it to make purchases using your credit card.

1

Press the Home key to continue

B008A0A0

Registering in this way not only lets you buy books, but also send documents to your Kindle over email, and send books from Amazon's site using a regular browser rather than the Kindle.

Walkthrough

Skill level	Beginner – a simple task that everyone can complete
Time required	Around five minutes
Equipment	Kindle, Kindle Paperwhite, Kindle Keyboard or Kindle Fire. Mac or PC with a network connection and Internet browser

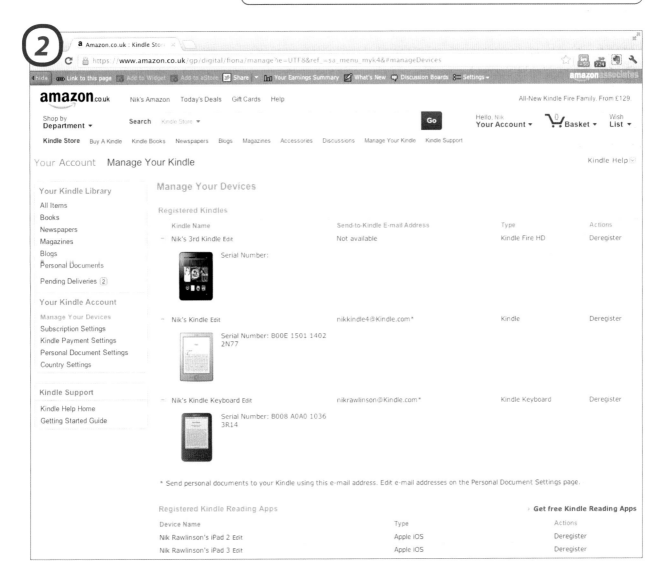

Keeping your Kindle password protected

Nobody wants to lose their Kindle; worse still to have it stolen. Neither of these is a pleasant scenario to consider but it's a sad truth of life that no matter how careful you are with your possessions there's always a chance they can go astray.

Fortunately Amazon makes it relatively easy to protect your Kindle and its contents so that even if you don't manage to recover it you can keep prying eyes away from any private and personal documents you have synced to it.

This is done by applying a password, which can be as simple or as complex as you like. When in place it will prevent anyone from reading your books and any personal documents you've sent to the device and – more importantly – stop them from buying anything on your account. With any luck, so long as you don't choose a very obvious password, it should delay them for long enough to give you a chance to change the password on your Amazon account and deregister the Kindle remotely.

There's still no way to locate a lost Kindle remotely, so you might never get it back, so it still pays to keep a close eye on it.

Walkthrough

Skill level	Beginner – a simple task that everyone can complete
Time required	Around five minutes
Equipment	Kindle, Kindle Paperwhite, Kindle Keyboard or Kindle Fire. Mac or PC with a network connection and Internet browser

---

Setting a password

---

1. Click the menu button and select Settings. Press the page forward button to advance to the next screen. Move down to Device Password and click the centre button.

2. Enter a password that you'll find easy to remember but anyone else would find hard to guess. You should try to use a mixture of letters and symbols or numbers here and avoid common combinations like QWERTY, 12345 or 'password'. On the Kindle Keyboard, use the Sym button to switch to these; on the Kindle and Kindle Paperwhite use the tabbed keyboard to switch to other letter sets. When you have entered a password, add a hint that will help you recall what it is if you later forget it (*see right*).

3. The next time you switch on your Kindle – and every time thereafter until you deactivate the password – you'll be asked to enter it before you can do anything. If you have forgotten what your password is, press the down button on the four-way controller. This will reveal your hint, as well as the contact numbers you'll need to phone to get Amazon to reset the device if you've forgotten the password.

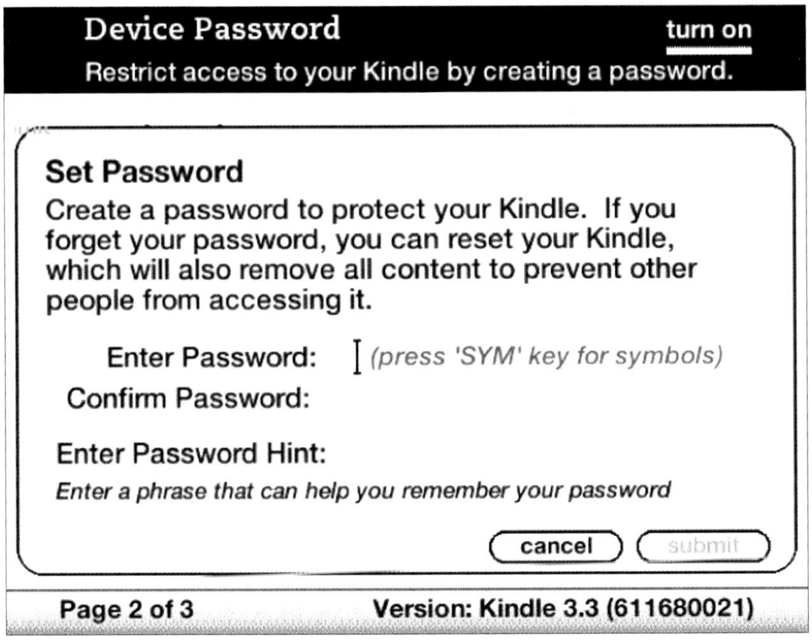

Device Password   **turn on**
Restrict access to your Kindle by creating a password.

Set Password
Create a password to protect your Kindle. If you forget your password, you can reset your Kindle, which will also remove all content to prevent other people from accessing it.

    Enter Password: ❘ *(press 'SYM' key for symbols)*
    Confirm Password:

Enter Password Hint:
Enter a phrase that can help you remember your password

          (cancel) (submit)

Page 2 of 3   **Version: Kindle 3.3 (611680021)**

Removing a Kindle from your Amazon account

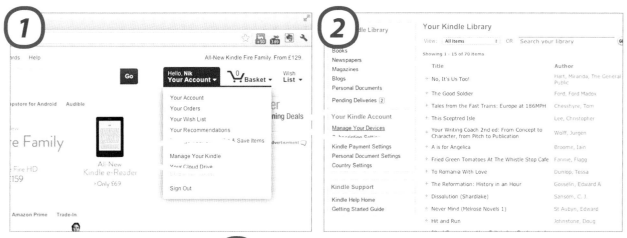

Should you lose a Kindle, the first thing you should do is remove it from your account. You should do exactly the same if you decide to sell it on. Why? Because deregistering removes it from your account and stops the person you sold it to – or someone who may have stolen or found it on the bus – from buying books using your payment details. It also stops any documents you might have set up to be emailed to your device from reaching their destination.

It's easiest to do this using a regular browser – which is obviously the only way you can do it if the device has been stolen. Log in to Amazon as usual and click the *Your Account* link above the search bar, then pick *Manage Your Kindle* from the menu.

Click *Manage Your Devices* in the sidebar to open a list of all the Kindle hardware devices that you own and have previously registered to your account, along with any Kindle reader applications installed on smartphones, tablets, Macs or PCs and any pre-ordered Kindles that haven't yet arrived.

Click the *Deregister* link beside each of the devices you want to remove from your account. Amazon will warn you that you should only deregister a device if you're passing it on and that it will no longer be able to purchase new books on your account. Click *Deregister* to confirm the action.

Reading with your Kindle

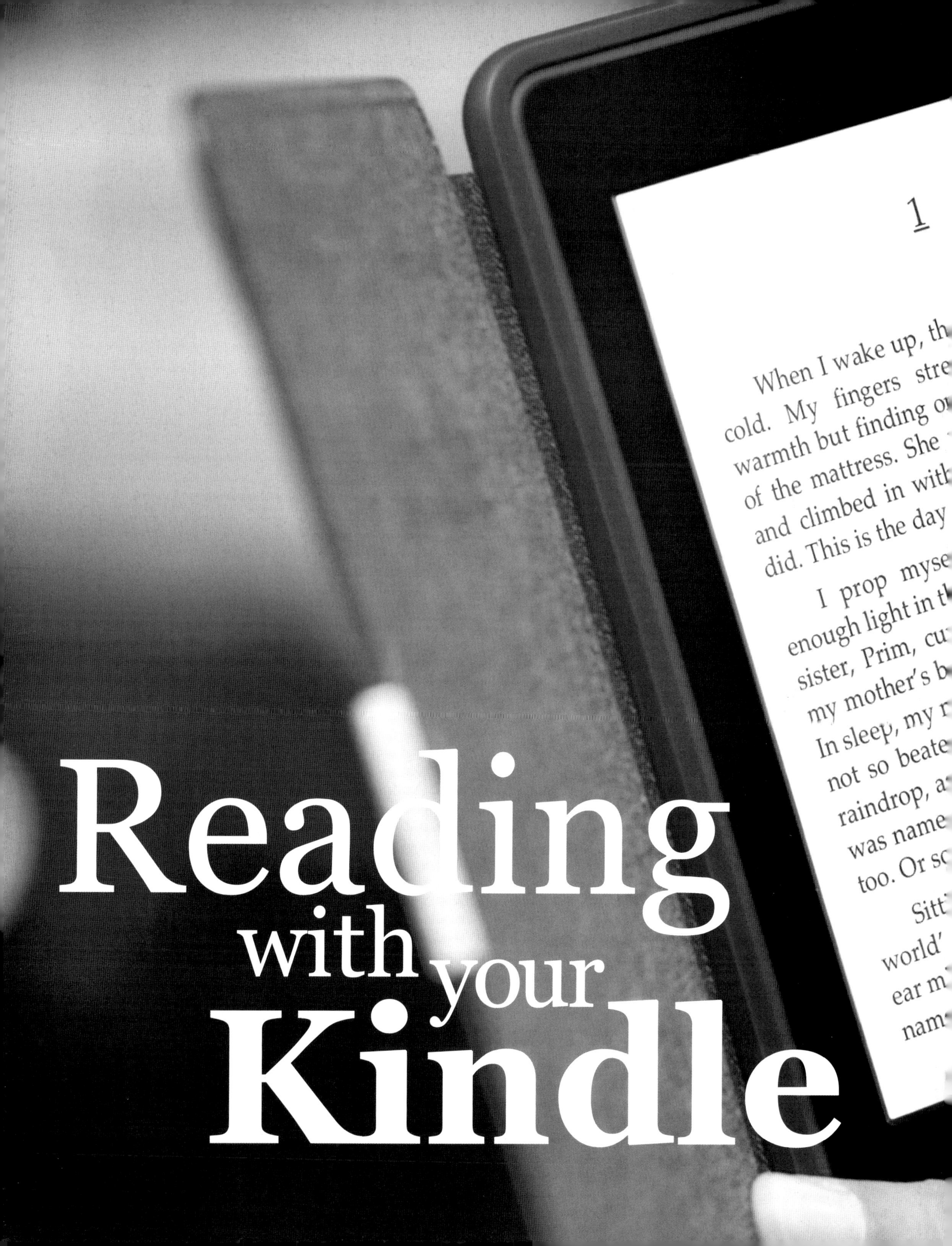

side of the bed is

, seeking Prim's

ough canvas cover

ve had bad dreams

other. Of course, she

eaping.

on one elbow. There's

om to see them. My little

on her side, cocooned in

eir cheeks pressed together.

ooks younger, still worn but

. Prim's face is as fresh as a

as the primrose for which she

nother was very beautiful once,

ll me.

rim's knees, guarding her, is the

t cat. Mashed-in nose, half of one

eyes the color of rotting squash. Prim

Buttercup, insisting that his muddy

kindle

Buying books directly using your Kindle

One of the best things about the Kindle platform is its simplicity. No Kindle device ever needs to be attached to your PC or Mac before it's put to use, and you don't need either of those computers to download books. If you bought it from Amazon it will even arrive set up and ready to go, with your Amazon account details already programmed in. You then quite simply unbox the product, charge it up, switch it on and go.

Amazon's dedicated Kindle Store is built right in to each Kindle device, with an option on the main menu taking you to the store to search for books. Although you can't buy Kindle versions of every book published, the catalogue of available titles is extensive and impressive, and there are several hundred volumes that are available *only* on the Kindle and not in print. To make it easier to shop through your device, Amazon doesn't include any print publications in the version of the store built in to the Kindle. If you want to browse them you'll have to use a regular computer, or the Kindle's integrated web browser.

Many Kindle books are cheaper than their regular paper-based editions, on account of the fact that producing them is cheaper and the publishers don't also have to pay for them to be shipped around the world. That means that by building up a digital, rather than paper library, you can make a decent saving. Do shop carefully, though, as this isn't always the case and, particularly if you're happy to buy second hand, you can sometimes find physical formats of the same titles for less money.

Here we'll walk you through the process of buying a book directly from your Kindle without the use of a computer as an interim platform. Over the pages that follow we'll show you how to do the same without a wireless connection, and how to send books directly from the Amazon store through a regular web browser. Whichever method you use, you really can be reading books in 60 second, just as Amazon promises.

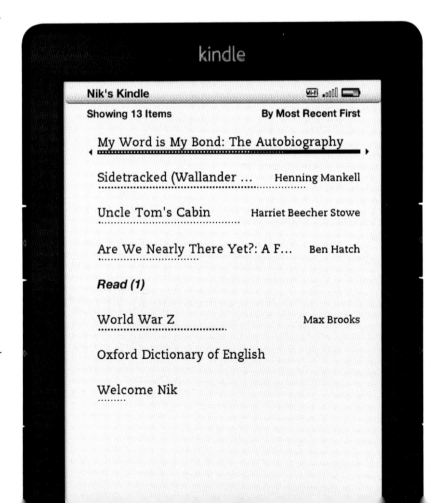

Skill level	Beginner – a simple task that everyone can complete
Time required	Around five minutes
Equipment	Kindle, Kindle Paperwhite, Kindle Keyboard or Kindle Fire, including previous-generation devices

Buying books on your Kindle

1. Make sure your Kindle is connected to your network by switching on wifi or using 3G. Press the menu button and select *Shop in Kindle Store* to visit Amazon's optimised shop containing only Kindle books through the built-in browser. You won't see any of the surrounding page furniture, but you can still access recommendations courtesy of Amazon's Kindle Post newsletter, which appears on the front page.

   Use the search box at the bottom of the screen to enter the title of your book, the name of a chosen author or keywords relating to the subject you want to read about. Press the centre button to perform the search, and after a moment's hesitation Kindle returns a list of results.

(1) lik's Kindle

amazon.co.uk

Browse:

Books   Blogs

Newspapers

Magazines

Kindle Bestsellers - *The Hanging Shed*

New & Noteworthy Books - *The Payback*

Kindle Post Mon, March 14, 2011 9:36 AM GMT

The Independent
Katy Guest on *A Widow's Story* by Joyce Carol Oates: "This is the first memoir that Oates/Smith has written, and it is...

Recommended for You

See All

my word is my bond   search store

2. When you've found the book you were looking for you can either buy it directly or download the first few pages for free. Do the latter by moving the selector to the *Try a Sample* line and pressing the centre button. The sample will download automatically at no charge for you to preview.

3. You'll be able to read around 5% of the book in this free sample. When you get to the end of the excerpt you can either keep it and take no action or, if you enjoyed it, download the rest of the book. Do this by moving the pointer to the *Buy Now* link at the end of the sample file and clicking the centre button. If your Kindle is still connected you will be charged an the book will download.

4. When the download completes your book will be added to the top of your home screen. The sample will remain on your device, so if you want to be tidy and remove it, move the underline up to its entry, press right on the four-way controller and select Delete.

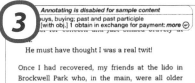

How to buy books through your PC or Mac browser

Good though the Kindle's built-in Store access is, it's not always the most convenient route through which to buy book digital books. If you'd prefer a more leisurely shopping experience, and you have access to a regular computer with an active internet connection you might instead want to do your shopping through a full browser and send your books to your Kindle over the air from there. Here we'll show you how to do just that in four simple steps.

Walkthrough

Skill level	Beginner – a simple task that everyone can complete
Time required	Around five minutes
Equipment	Any Kindle, including previous versions, or a PC or Mac with an Internet connection

Step by Step

1. Open your browser and visit the local Amazon store for your country. Use the links on the left of the homepage to visit the Kindle Store, selecting *Kindle eBooks* from the fly-out menu. Click in the search box at the top of the page and enter the title of the book you want to read, the name of a favourite author or keywords that describe the subject you're looking for.

2. Select the book you want from the list of results to call up a full description, an image of its cover and any reviews left behind by previous readers.

3. Use the drop-down menu on the right of the screen to select the device to which you want to send the book. This list includes not only regular Kindle hardware devices but also Kindle applications that you've installed on mobile devices such as the iPhone or iPad, and the reader applications for use on PCs and Macs.

4. Open the Kindle menu and select *Sync & Check for Items* to download the book you sent from your browser. You can also send samples by using the *Try it free* drop-down.

How to transfer books to your Kindle using USB

Over the next few pages we'll be exploring alternatives to the regular Kindle Store. Not only does expanding the number of shops from which you buy content increase your choice of books, but it means you can often find books for free that aren't stocked on the Kindle Store. If you have downloaded books through your browser rather than through Amazon's own store you'll need to transfer them to your Kindle manually by connecting it to your PC or Mac and dragging them across.

Walkthrough

Skill level	Beginner – a simple task that everyone can complete
Time required	Around five minutes
Equipment	Any Kindle, including previous versions, and a PC or Mac with a vacant USB port, plus bundled Kindle USB cable

Step by Step

1. Start by connecting your Kindle to your PC or Mac. Ideally you should connect it to a powered port physically attached to your computer, unless any additional external hub connected to your computer has its own power supply. If you've lost the cable that came with your Kindle and need to buy a new one, search Amazon using the term *'usb cable for kindle'* to view authorised replacements. However, it uses a standard plug, so also check any other USB devices you own to see whether their connectors are compatible, but never force one that doesn't fit easily.

2. Your Kindle will appear on either your PC or Mac as though it was an external hard drive, with the name Kindle. Here we are using a Mac.

3. Drag your downloaded Kindle or Mobipocket format book into the folder to send it to your device. It now appears at the top of your home screen.

Open a Finder or Windows Explorer window and click the Kindle and open the *'documents'* folder.

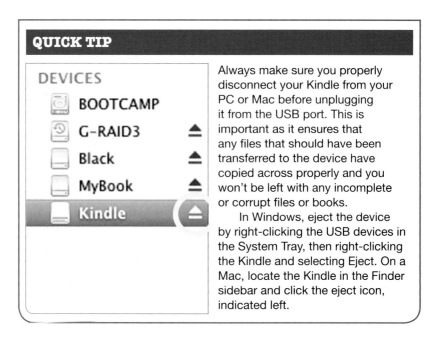

QUICK TIP

DEVICES

BOOTCAMP
G-RAID3
Black
MyBook
Kindle

Always make sure you properly disconnect your Kindle from your PC or Mac before unplugging it from the USB port. This is important as it ensures that any files that should have been transferred to the device have copied across properly and you won't be left with any incomplete or corrupt files or books.

In Windows, eject the device by right-clicking the USB devices in the System Tray, then right-clicking the Kindle and selecting Eject. On a Mac, locate the Kindle in the Finder sidebar and click the eject icon, indicated left.

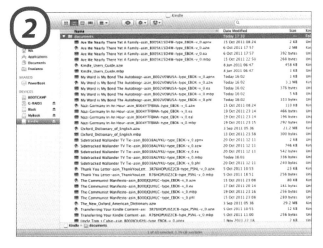

Alternative bookstores

Although **Amazon's own** store is certainly the most convenient place to shop, on account of being intimately tied to the Kindle itself and even appearing in the Kindle menus, there are plenty of alternative sources well worth checking out.

By shopping around you can often make savings as it means you can download cheaper versions of the same books, and in some cases enjoy wider choice as Amazon's extensive catalogue certainly doesn't include every book converted for Kindle reading.

Here we'll profile the best places to buy and find out about books outside of Amazon's walled garden. If you want to go hunting for further options then make sure the books you download are either dedicated .AZW Kindle files, or Mobipocket-formatted books. Amazon's own format is a variation on Mobipocket.

Sadly the widely-used ePub format, which was adopted by Apple as the basis of its own iBook Store, Sony for its Reader Store and Kobo for its own online shop, isn't compatible with the Kindle, despite hints that the latest-but-one raft of hardware devices would indeed read and render the format.

Don't be tempted to copy paid-for books from friends and family. Not only is this unfair on the authors who in many cases have spent years working on their tomes (and it's illegal), but there's a good chance you'll find that the books won't work on your device.

Most books downloaded from Amazon and other online bookstores include digital rights management (DRM) code that ties them to the account of the person who bought them. If that isn't you, they won't work on your Kindle, wasting you both time and space.

Left: Open any book's dedicated page from the Gutenberg results for a choice of formats. Choose Kindle if available, and plain text or Mobipocket if not to download a version that's compatible with your device.

Project Gutenberg
www.gutenberg.org

Gutenberg is the king of all alternative online book resources. At the time of writing it contains over 40,000 books in a wide range of formats in languages as diverse as Esperanto, Breton and Occitan. All of them have one thing in common: they are out of copyright in the US, and so as long as you're not infringing any copyright regulations in your own country you're free to download them.

Project Gutenberg was established by Michael S Hart on 4th July 1971. Appropriately enough, considering the date, the first work he entered into the project's now vast collection, was the Declaration of Independence. At the time he wanted the complete catalogue to eventually hold at least 10,000 of the most commonly consulted books so that they could be accessed and used by anyone for free (although donations are always welcome).

It was a noble cause that over the years has received significant donations and now far exceeds its original stated aims, with an average of 50 new books being added to the database every week.

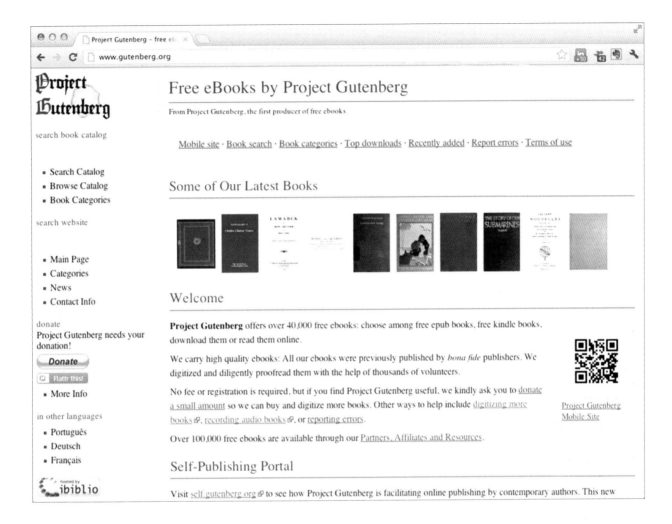

The most commonly-published language on the site is English, followed in turn by French, German and Finnish.

Project Gutenberg has a comprehensive search tool allowing you to interrogate the catalogue in a similar manner to Amazon itself, and it maintains a list of newly-added content and most popular downloads if you need a quick fix. This is the best place to look if you're after literature and classics, as titles like *Ulysses*, *Jane Eyre* and *Pride and Prejudice* are habitual inhabitants on the list.

To download a book, click its title to open its dedicated record and then choose the format you're after. The simplest of all formats is Plain Text, which is fully compatible with the Kindle, but for the best experience you should choose the Kindle (no images) format if it's offered. Avoid choosing ePub as this won't work on the Kindle – it's intended for alternative hardware readers, and many e-reader apps installed on tablets and smartphones.

Click the appropriate format and if it's one that your browser can't render within its own window it will be downloaded to your computer (you can't send them direct to your Kindle). If you find that the file opens directly then it's one that your browser is able to read (this is commonly the case with plain text files). In this instance, either hold shift while clicking to save it to your hard drive in a default location, or right-click the link and select the option to save it if you want to also be able to choose the location where it is stored.

You'll find that the quality of the books varies, although in general they're all very well produced and, due to the large number of distributed proofreaders helping out around the world, are generally accurate copies of the original work. They are fully compatible with the Kindle's various options for changing font faces and text size, although obviously you can't remove elements like double spaces (*see below*) that shouldn't be there.

Note that is the case with many of the books you can download from these alternative outlets the Gutenberg files won't include the embedded page numbers that you can find in some Kindle files downloaded from Amazon, so although this is a great way to join in with a reading group for free you may find that it's more discuss the classics if the group is using specific page references.

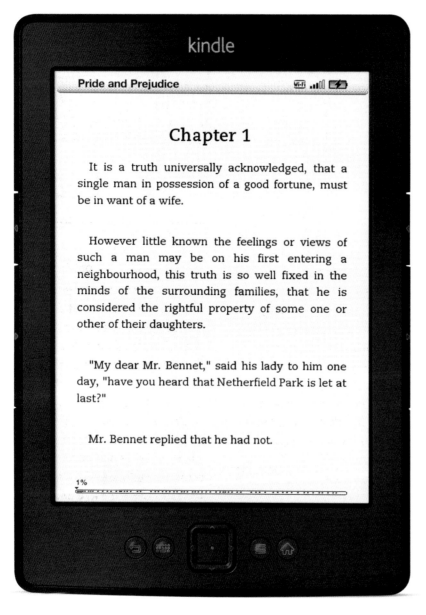

JOHANNES GUTENBERG

Gutenberg, after whom the project is named, is famed for having invented the modern printing press. Living in Mainz the early 15th century, his innovation was so-called movable type, which allowed the various parts of a page – the letters, numbers and so on – to be moved around and re-used between jobs. The biggest and most famous book printed this way was the Gutenberg Bible, of which 21 copies survive.

Image: Wikipedia

Left: All books are added to the Project Gutenberg catalogue by volunteers and although quality is generally very good stylistic points will vary between the different titles on offer.

Open Library
www.openlibrary.org

The goal of Open Library is to produce a single web page for every book ever published. By its own admission this adds up to 'hundreds of millions of book records'.

Each book's record includes a short review, a picture of the cover and details of each edition published – both digital and physical. These are linked directly to the shops through which you can buy them including Alibris, Amazon, AbeBooks and Book Depository. For our needs, Amazon is naturally of greatest interest.

So why would you choose to find books this way rather than buy them directly through Amazon? Because it's the easiest way to find out more about your book before you set out to read it. On Amazon you can read the publisher's blurb and, often, reader reviews. Through Open Library, on the other hand, you'll also find excerpts from Wikipedia, information about the different imprints and reprints and comment from such notable experts as Margaret Atwood, and an extensive system of tags and links that put each book in context for a richer buying experience.

All of the content on the Open Library is open source, from the written words to the underlying code. Like Wikipedia it relies to a great degree on input from a community of volunteers who write and edit each entry. If you find it of use, then, do your bit and help out by adding some details for the last book you enjoyed.

Feedbooks
www.feedbooks.com

Although Feedbooks' commercial titles aren't compatible with the hardware Kindle readers or their equivalent apps and software installations, its public domain books will work on them. Many of these titles are the same as the books you can find on Project Gutenberg, but the process of searching and downloading through Feedbooks (*left*) is much more pleasant thanks to a well thought-out interface. It may well be the most successful store you've never heard of, distributing 3,000,000 books a month.

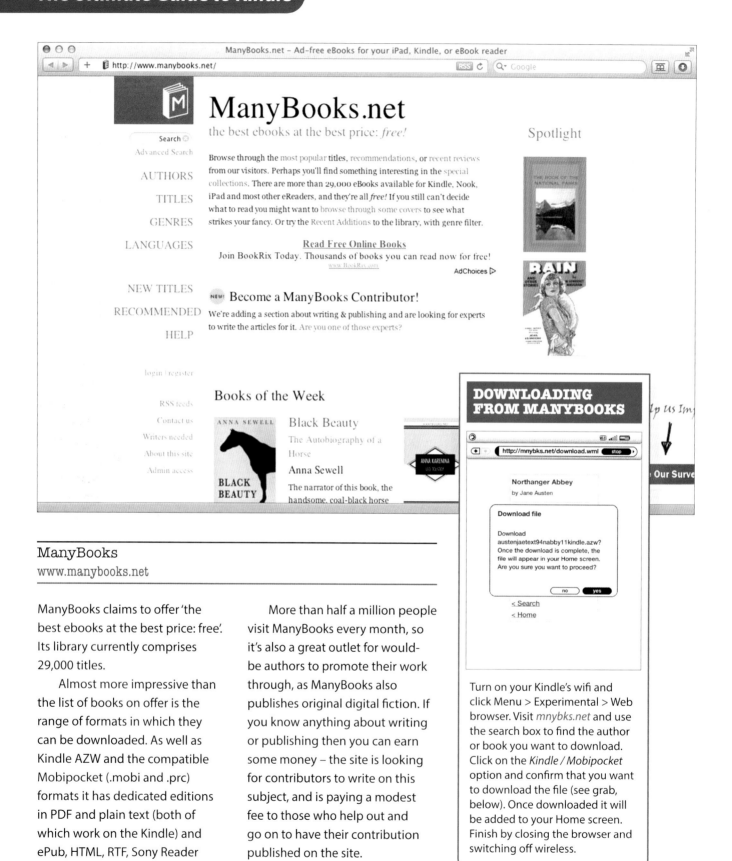

ManyBooks
www.manybooks.net

ManyBooks claims to offer 'the best ebooks at the best price: free'. Its library currently comprises 29,000 titles.

Almost more impressive than the list of books on offer is the range of formats in which they can be downloaded. As well as Kindle AZW and the compatible Mobipocket (.mobi and .prc) formats it has dedicated editions in PDF and plain text (both of which work on the Kindle) and ePub, HTML, RTF, Sony Reader and more.

More than half a million people visit ManyBooks every month, so it's also a great outlet for would-be authors to promote their work through, as ManyBooks also publishes original digital fiction. If you know anything about writing or publishing then you can earn some money – the site is looking for contributors to write on this subject, and is paying a modest fee to those who help out and go on to have their contribution published on the site.

Turn on your Kindle's wifi and click Menu > Experimental > Web browser. Visit *mnybks.net* and use the search box to find the author or book you want to download. Click on the *Kindle / Mobipocket* option and confirm that you want to download the file (see grab, below). Once downloaded it will be added to your Home screen. Finish by closing the browser and switching off wireless.

O'Reilly Media
oreilly.com

O'Reilly is one of the leading publishers of technical non-fiction books in the world. Its titles have long been trusted by those who work with computers and web technology as some of the most reliable texts on a wide variety of subjects, and its policy where ebooks are concerned is very liberal and forward-thinking. For starters, it doesn't apply digital rights management measures to its work, meaning there's nothing to stop you from installing them on several of your devices.

It publishes in a wide variety of formats, which have been optimised for different platforms (it publishes in Mobipocket format for Kindle-using customers), and it also provides free updates for life, so you know that even if you buy a book today and it receives an update tomorrow you'll be able to download the amendments, too,

so that your book stays current and relevant. At the opposite end of the scale, 'early release' versions are unedited books that the company is still working on, which are nonetheless available to buy so that you can get a heads-up on the latest technology, and received the edited version for free when it's finished.

Check in at the site frequently as it runs deals of the day, so if the book you're after isn't on offer now there's a chance it could be before too long.

Below: O'Reilly's ebooks are keenly priced and can be bought alongside the print editions.

QUICK TIP

Don't forget to check out Amazon's constantly updated lists of most popular books. There are two of these: both paid-for titles and free volumes, each of which can be accessed from the homepage of the Store.

If you're feeling guilty about not being better read in the classics, head for the freebies first as many of the best-loved books of all time are now out of copyright and are free to download. It makes a lot more sense to catch up on what you're missed in this way than to head to a regular shop and pay for a physical copy.

Listening to audiobooks

As we'll show you later, sound-enabled Kindles can read books aloud, using the text and its integrated speech synthesiser to translate the content into spoken word.

If you have a Kindle Keyboard, Kindle 1, 2 or 3, or Kindle DX you can go one stage further and also play back original spoken word books for which you don't own the text edition, courtesy of downloads from Audible.

Audible books use a specific format that makes them far more flexible and versatile than regular MP3 files. Your Kindle will be able to remember where you left off when you were last listening to one, and you can skip backwards and forwards to specific points. With MP3s, all you can do is play them in the background while you're reading your book.

Audible sells audiobooks in a number of audio formats, with formats 2 and 3, which are compatible with the first generation Kindle, equivalent to AM and FM radio respectively. Format 4, which is compatible with the first, second and third generation Kindles, plus Kindle DX, is roughly equivalent to an average MP3. Audible Enhanced Audio-formatted files have sound quality equivalent to a CD, and are compatible only with the Kindle DX and second and third-generation devices, including Kindle Keyboard.

Transferring content

Compatible Kindles have an *'audible'* folder ready for you to drop in your content (if yours doesn't and it's listed above, you can create it by plugging the Kindle into your Mac or PC and using the Finder or Explorer).

You can only play back Audible files with the .aa or .aac extension. Dropping in any others will have no effect as they won't show up on your Home screen.

Below: Kindle Keyboard users, and anyone with an older Kindle device, can buy audiobooks from Audible and play them back using their device's integrated player. Audible is an Amazon company, so it's not surprising that you can link your Amazon and Audible accounts.

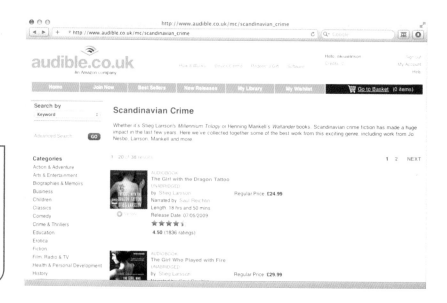

KEYBOARD CONTROL

Rather than using the graphical controls on the bottom of the Kindle display, Kindle Keyboard owners can use alt-F to skip to the next track, and alt-space to pause and resume playback.

Rapid Spanish: Volume 1

Rapid Spanish: Volume 1
by Earworms Learning

Narrator: Marlon Lodge
Date: 15-Jul-2005
Length: 1 hr. 11 min. 49 sec.

0:01:50   Section 1 of 11

Page 1 of 1

Left: Audible files are encoded in a way that makes them more flexible than MP3s. Many Kindles can use this encoding to offer a full set of playback controls.

pressing the central button when you reach the one you want to use.

If this is the first time you have played an Audible file on your Kindle it will ask you to authorise your device by entering your Audible username and password. If you can't remember what these are, visit *audible.com* or *audible.co.uk*, click Sign in and use the *Forgotten your username or password?* link to retrieve them. Note that your audible password isn't the same as your Amazon password or any password you have set on your Kindle to prevent it being used when lost or stolen.

You will only need to authorise your device once and it will then play all of your compatible previous purchases on your Kindle.

Audible books are sold through Audible's own site at *audible.com* and *audible.co.uk*.

Playing audio files

Having successfully transferred your content, eject your Kindle and disconnect it from your computer. You'll see the new file on the Home screen, with an 'audible' tag in the margin to show that it is an audio file and distinguish it from your books or samples. Open it and use the four-way controller's centre button to click the Play button, or use the left and right controls on that same controller to move between the various on-screen buttons of the transport bar,

QUICK TIP

Not all Audible files are shipped in format 4, so shop carefully. In particular pay attention when buying Audible files through third-party retailers, which may not specify the format on offer.

Highlighting text and posting to social networks

You can't scribble in the margins of a digital book, so Amazon has implemented a clever system of notes and highlights, which allow you to perform a similar task using your Kindle's keyboard controls.

However, it's take on note-making is smarter than a regular pen and a printed book could ever be, as these highlights and favourite sections can also be shared with your Twitter followers and Facebook friends by posting them directly to your tweet stream or Wall from the Kindle itself.

Highlighting text

A true bookworm enjoys not just the story, but also the style of the writing contained within its pages. Few who fall into this category can resist the urge to make a note of their favourite passages so that they can come back to them in the future, but without easily accessible page numbers or the option of turning down a corner you might think that was easier said than done where Kindle books were concerned.

Fortunately not. Every time you come across a notable passage, use the four-way controller on

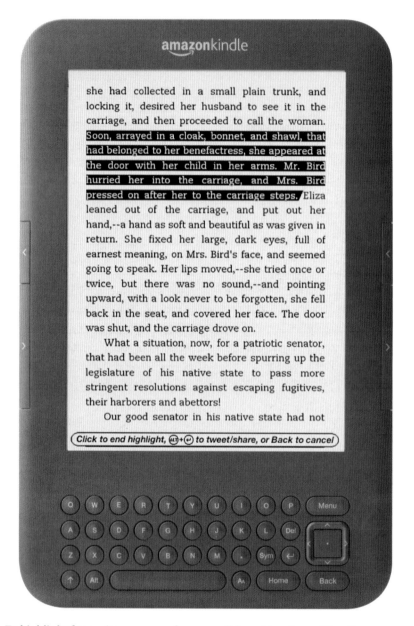

To highlight favourite passages from a well-loved book, position the cursor at the start of the passage, press the centre button and then move to the furthest end of the passage before pressing the button again to save it.

Above: As well as being underlined on the Kindle copy of each book, popular highlights are displayed on Amazon's book listing pages.

the Kindle and Kindle Keyboard to move to the start and press the centre button, or touch the screen on the Kindle Paperwhite. Now move the cursor through the text until you get to the end of the passage. Press the centre button again to save the highlight.

Retrieving your jottings

Your highlights and notes are stored alongside your book and automatically backed up on Amazon's servers (you can turn this off through *Settings | Annotations Backup | turn off*). You can retrieve them by pressing Menu while reading any page of the book and selecting *View Notes & Marks*, where they'll be organised into a table in page order.

Popular highlights

If you have chosen to share your highlights with other readers, Amazon will amalgamate them anonymously, along with everyone else's and sync them along with every copy of the book to which they relate on every device to which it has been downloaded.

These highlights have a feint dotted underline below them in the flow of the book, at the start of which is a note of how many people have chosen to mark it out (*see below left*). If you find this annoying, turn off the popular highlights feature by opening *Settings*, turning to the second (Kindle Keyboard) or third page (Kindle / Kindle Paperwhite) and clicking the *turn off* link beside Popular Highlights. Just below this you'll also find the link to turn off Public Notes, which are those notes written by people that you follow at *kindle.amazon.com*. These differ from highlights in

Left: To hide popular highlights, press return while viewing the page on which they appear. Turn them off permanently through Settings.

There are in this world blessed souls, whose
sorrows all spring up into joys for others; whose
earthly hopes, laid in the grave with many tears,
are the seed from which spring healing flowers
and balm for the desolate and the distressed.
Among such was the delicate woman who sits
there by the lamp, dropping slow tears, while she
prepares the memorials of her own lost one for the
outcast wanderer.

630 highlighters

that highlights are merely marked out passages of the original text, which are displayed on your device whether you follow the people who marked them out or not. Notes, on the other hand, will only be displayed if they were made by someone you actively follow.

If you don't want to turn off the number of popular highlights permanently, pressing the central button hides them on the current page.

Sharing your highlights with your Twitter followers

Whether it's because you want to prove how well read you are, or you just want to inspire your friends to pick up a book you've enjoyed, Kindle also lets you share your favourite passages with your Twitter and Facebook followers using its built-in tools.

Walkthrough

Skill level	Intermediate – generally easy, but requires some supplementary account details
Time required	Around five minutes
Equipment	Kindle, Kindle Paperwhite, Kindle Keyboard or Kindle Fire. Includes previous-generation devices. Twitter account

Set up Kindle to post to Twitter

1. Open *Settings | Social Networks | Manage*. Kindle activates its integrated browser at this point and opens a page, so make sure 3G or wifi are active on your device. Select Twitter as the service you want to authorise.
2. Enter your Twitter username and password and then click *Sign in* to authorise the application to post to your account (*see below*).
3. You'll be logged in to Twitter and then directed back to the set-up screen which will confirm that the process has completed by displaying your Twitter username within the Twitter section.

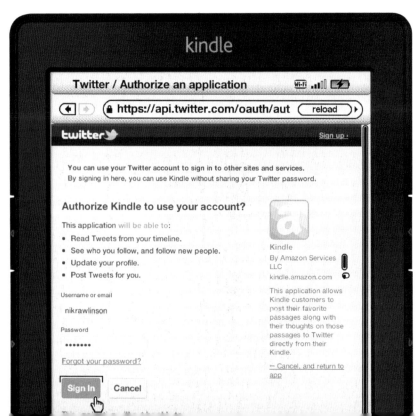

Walkthrough

Skill level	Intermediate – generally easy, but requires some supplementary account details
Time required	Around five minutes
Equipment	Kindle, Kindle Paperwhite, Kindle Keyboard or Kindle Fire. Includes previous-generation device. Facebook account

Set up Kindle to post to Facebook

1. Repeat step 1 from the Twitter walkthrough, this time choosing to authorise Facebook instead.
2. Use your email address or phone number to log in to Facebook, remembering that the @ symbol is found behind the SYM button on the Kindle Keyboard, and on the secondary on-screen keyboards on Kindle and Kindle Paperwhite.
3. In an effort to improve security, Facebook likes to register each device you use to access its services. Choose a logical name for your Kindle (we've chosen 'kindle keyboard', below) and then confirm that you want it to access your basic information and data and post to Facebook as though it was you by clicking Allow on the following screen.

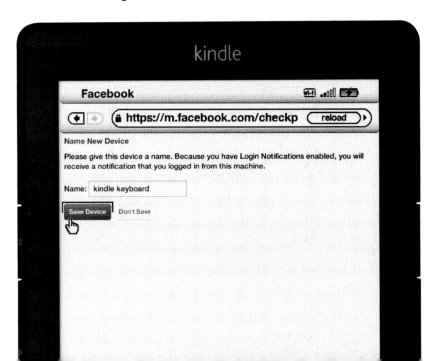

To do this it obviously requires that you have your login details for each service to hand, so with wifi or 3G active on your device, open Settings and follow the instructions in the two walkthroughs to the left.

You can now share content from your book using either social network, remembering at all times to respect any copyright regulations that may be applicable, such as sharing only a small part for the purpose of evaluation or review.

To do this, repeat the process of highlighting your chosen passage by clicking at the start and end of the selected text, and then hold alt while pressing return to share it to either network. Kindle will ask you to add a short note which will be appended to your highlight. When you've done this, click the on-screen 'share' button. If wifi or 3G are turned on (it'll warn you if they aren't) it will post your covering note to either or both of your social networks, depending on which you have set up, along with a link to the highlighted text, which will be stored on *kindle. amazon.com*. Linking in this way rather than including it directly allows you to highlight more than Twitter's 140 character limit.

How to back up your Kindle purchases

Keeping a local backup of your Kindle purchases will let you re-install them on your device without downloading them again from Amazon's servers in the event of a catastrophic crash.

Step by step

1. Connect your Kindle to your computer. What happens next depends on whether you're using a Mac or PC. On a Mac, the device appears in the Finder sidebar; on Windows it's assigned a drive letter. If your PC asks you what you'd like to do with the Kindle, simply choose to open it and it will be treated like an external drive.

2. You'll see three folders on your Kindle: *documents*, *audible* and *music*. The second and third of these contain audio books and MP3s. The first – *documents* – is where the Kindle saves your downloaded books. Double-click it to open up its contents. The files inside this folder aren't particularly well organised as your books, their metadata and any text files, PDFs and screen grabs are all bundled together. We only want to back up our books, so use the Mac's toolbar search box to filter it down to just .azw files, or click the drop-down menu on the right hand side of the Type column header in Windows and select AZW as the displayed file type.

You can now drag these isolated files to another location on your computer to back them up. This will save only the books themselves. If you want to also save your bookmarks then you should also make a copy of any files bearing the same name with a .mbp extension. Store them on a hard drive or flash

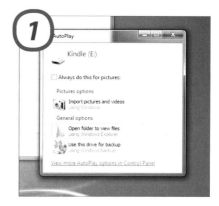

AMAZON DRM

Although you can copy books from your Kindle to local backups for repopulating your device without redownloading all of your books, the digital rights management (DRM) built in to each one means you can't share them with others.

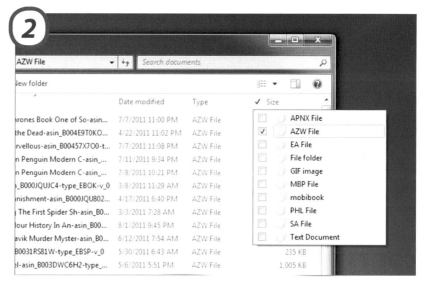

drive, but don't be tempted to share them with friends. Not only is it illegal to share books in this way, but Amazon has implemented a digital rights management system that will prevent them from working on any Kindle that is not registered to your account.

3. Should you have a problem with your Kindle that causes it to lose your books, you can copy them back over USB. However, to read them on an alternative device or an app you'll have to send new copies to each one. Do this either by browsing through archived items on your Kindle or by logging in to Amazon and selecting *Your Account | Manage your Kindle*. This calls your past purchases with buttons beside each one that send purchased books to an alternative device.

4. You can also transfer books by USB, which allows you to save money by buying a wifi Kindle even if you don't have a wireless network. To do this, select Transfer by Computer when buying a book and again select the destination device.

Walkthrough

Skill level	Intermediate – requires some familiarity with Windows or the Mac
Time required	Around ten minutes
Equipment	Any Kindle plus a Mac or PC and the bundled Kindle USB cable

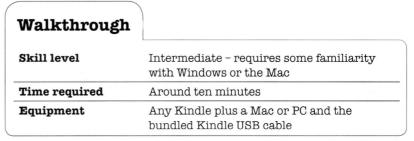

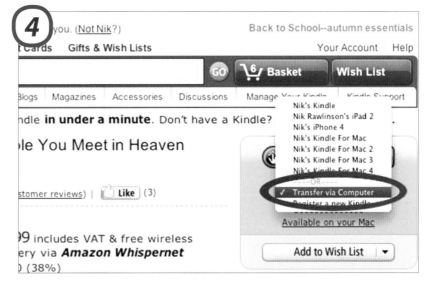

Reading Kindle books... without using your Kindle

Amazon no doubt turns a tidy profit from the Kindle, but the real money is in books. For every Kindle it sells, it'll have to take off the cost of research, design, production and shipping it out to customers around the world.

With an ebook, though, its takings are almost all profit, which is why Amazon can afford to pay its publishers such a generous share of the royalties. All it needs to do is host the book file on its cloud servers and deliver it to the reader whenever they request a copy. The first time they do, the cost of delivery is deducted from the publisher's share of the takings.

It's no wonder, then, that Amazon has sought to push its Kindle technology onto as many platforms as possible, with native applications for the iPad and iPhone, Android, Macs and PCs.

Unfortunately for Amazon, Apple changed the rules on in-app purchases for all applications hosted on the iPhone or iPad, dictating that all such purchases should be handled by its own payment processing mechanism, with cards linked to its own online store used as the payment mechanism.

Clearly this was unacceptable to Amazon for two reasons. First, it meant that it lost its direct relationship with its customers, so would find it more difficult to make recommendations to each of us about which books we might enjoy in the future on the basis of what we've bought in the past. Second, the 30% that Apple was demanding in exchange for processing the purchase was exactly the same as the amount that Amazon took from the sale of each book from publishers.

Below: Native apps let you read Kindle purchases on a Mac or PC

Apple gave its app developers a fair amount of notice that it intended to implement this process, and that applications which didn't comply could no longer be sold through its online store. So, Amazon developed new apps for Apple's mobile devices, without the Kindle Store, submitted them for approval and at the same time built a browser-based reader, now hosted at *read. amazon.com*

This boasts many of the same features as the dedicated applications, and of course has a link to the Kindle section of Amazon's online store.

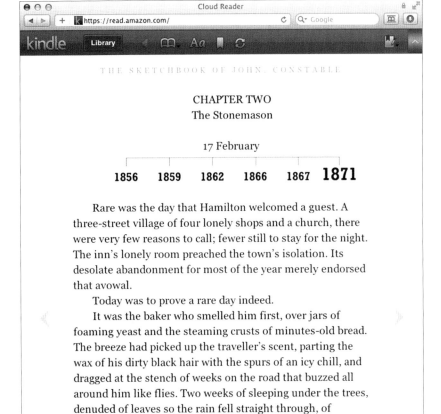

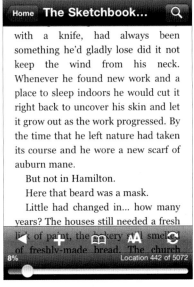

Above: The web-hosted Kindle reader gives you access to your complete library from anywhere in the world where you can get to a web connection. Above right: The Kindle iPhone app omits the direct buying feature.

The browser reader obviously also works on regular desktop and laptop computers, but if you prefer to use a native application then check the box of links, right, and download the Kindle apps for Windows and Mac users.

Unfortunately Amazon doesn't provide a Linux version of its Kindle software, despite the hardware Kindle devices running Linux as their underlying operating systems. Linux users should therefore use Wine.

DOWNLOAD LINKS

Download your reader application from the following sites:

Android phone
https://market.android.com/details?id=com.amazon.kindle

Blackberry
http://amazon.com/kindlebb

iPad and iPhone (universal app)
http://bit.ly/dY9Ooo

Windows XP, Vista or 7
http://amazon.com/gp/kindle/pc

Mac OS X
http://amazon.com/gp/kindle/mac (or from the Mac App Store at *http://bit.ly/sdSdab*)

Organising books on an e-ink Kindle

Even the most basic Kindle can hold 1,400 books at a time. That's a whole lifetime's worth of reading for most people. To carry the same number of regular books would be impossible without the help of some kind of transport.

This is a boon for avid readers, but it can make finding each one somewhat tricky – unless you organise them into collections.

Collections are virtual folders, and you can have several set up on your Kindle to handle different document types. So, you might want to create one for documents you've emailed to your Kindle, one books you want to read, another books you already have

read so that they don't clutter up the Home screen, a fourth for downloaded samples, and so on.

Filing a book in a collection

To add a book to a collection, return to the Home screen and then use the four-way controller to move down to the book you want to tidy away. Now press the right edge of the controller to call up the book options. The first of these is *Add to Collection...* Press the centre button to select it (*see grab, below*).

We've already created one collection on our Kindle, called Read, where we file books we have finished reading. At present,

as you can see from the image, it contains two books, as indicated by the number in brackets after its name (*see grab, below*). It's already selected, so we only need press the centre button again to file our new book into this folder alongside its existing residents.

If you would rather put your book in a different folder that you have already created, step down to it using the button of the four-way controller. If you want to start a new collection, step down to Create New Collection, press the centre button and give your new folder a name. When you confirm the name, the currently selected book will be automatically dropped inside it.

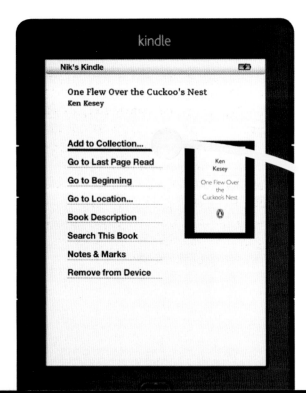

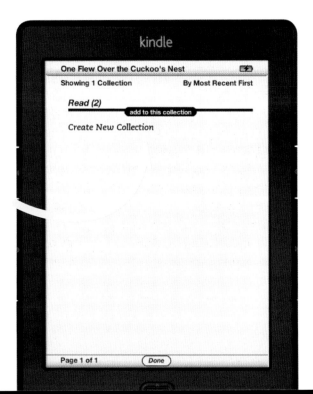

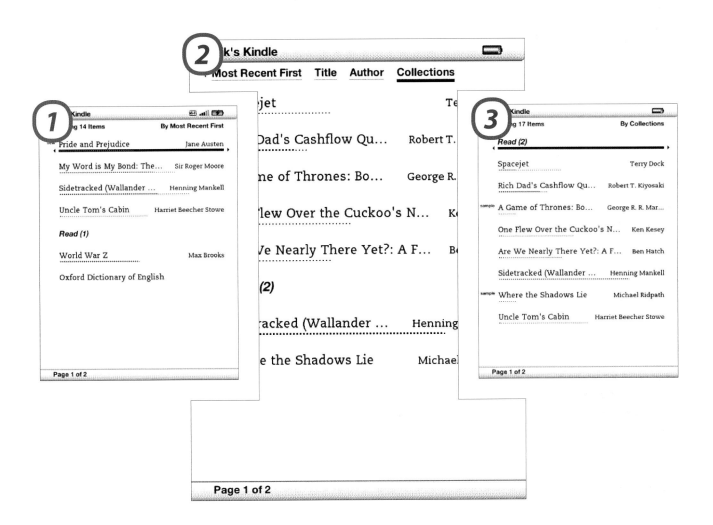

Using folders to organise the Home screen

By default your Kindle lists all of your books in order of use, with the most recently opened volume listed at the top of the Home screen. This makes it easy to return to a book at the start of your next reading session.

In this state it will display all of your filed documents and books on the Home screen as well as inside their constituent collections (*grab 1, above*). That's fine if you want to see everything at once, but rather misses out on one major benefit of using folders: the ability to view books and documents that match a particular criteria in isolation.

To change this, move the selection line up to the top of the screen and press right on the four-way controller, and change *Most Recent First* to *Collections* (*grab 2*).

Your Home screen will now be reorganised, with the books you have filed in your collections (books we've finished reading in this case) hidden away inside your collections, making those you still have to open easier to find without all the clutter (*grab 3*).

As you will have noticed when changing the filing order in step 2, you can also organise books on your home screen alphabetically by title or author name.

Kindle
Hacks

How to publish your own Kindle book

Now that you've got to grips with downloading books and reading them on your Kindle, it's time to consider taking things further.

Thanks to the Kindle and Amazon's organised, integrated, end-to-end distribution method that lets readers buy books directly on their devices you can now publish your own material directly to your audience without following the usual route of finding an agent

Below: Amazon's clearly organised distribution channel links its online store to your readers' Kindles, allowing you to sell your books to them directly.

who can represent you to the publishing industry and negotiate deals on your behalf. They might not like it, but at least you have less red tape to snip.

Clearly this means that you'll have to do more of the work yourself – and all of the promotion of your work, but as the person who understands what you have written better than anyone else it makes sense for you to take on this role in the first place. Just prepare yourself for the fact that it means you may have less time to get on with writing the second and third books in your best-selling saga.

Over the following pages we'll walk you through the steps

involved in putting together your first Kindle book and selling it through Amazon's online store.

Learning from the pros

Barry Eisler landed himself a $500,000 publishing deal. He knew right away what he should do: he talked it over with his family, then turned it down.

Eisler isn't alone in turning his back on traditional publishing. A New York Times bestselling author, he's set himself up as a self publisher, convinced by a growing body of evidence that he'll earn more that way than any established imprint could pay him.

KINDLE CONSIDERATIONS

The e-ink Kindle's screen isn't colour, and neither will it be any time soon. Speaking to shareholders in May 2010, Amazon CEO Jeff Bezos said that the colour units it had in its labs they were 'not ready for prime-time production'. For the moment, then, design two covers for your book – one colour version to display on Amazon's site, and a higher contrast, sharper monochrome edition to embed within the book. Make the Kindle edition 960 by 1280 pixels and it'll exactly fit the screen.

You can't lay out your ebook with the precision of a printed magazine. Your readers can choose their own font face and size, so aim for the lowest common denominator to guarantee the broadest compatibility: flowing text in a single column. Embed images within the flow of the text rather than floating them to one side, as without knowing the dimensions of the screen in use you can't accurately predict how they will interact with the text.

Complex formatting, such as the timeline at the start of each chapter in *The Sketchbook of John, Constable*, should be created as a flat graphic. Avoid trying to match any particular font. Kindle's default font is Caecilia, of which you can buy a single cut for as little as £25 (*http://bit.ly/e2Qmmg*), but how do you know your readers haven't switched to the sans-serif or condensed fonts, and they aren't reading it on a mobile device? Instead, choose the best font for the job, regardless of the surrounding text.

Eisler, like fellow author Joe Konrath, sees publishers' relevance diminishing in a rapidly-changing industry. 'We're the writers. We provide the content that is printed and distributed,' Konrath wrote in response to Eisler's comments. 'For hundreds of years, writers couldn't reach readers without publishers. We needed them. Now, suddenly, we don't. But publishers don't seem to be taking this Very Important Fact into account.'

The rise of ebooks, the US sales of which overtook paperbacks in early 2011, is putting old-school publishers out of their jobs – and their agents, and even bricks-and-mortar bookshops along with them – while ereaders like the Kindle and iPad are helping even novice authors to find an audience and make real money from writing.

Bypassing the print publishing cycle should lead not only to lower prices for the reader thanks to an increased level of competition between micro-publishers and a reduction in their overall costs as they don't need to invest in paper, ink and physically shipping books around the world, but also greater reader choice. For most people, their bestselling, ground breaking first novel remains unwritten not because of the effort involved in getting the words on the page, but through lack of faith that those pages will ever be read. Imagine what might happen if publication wasn't a possibility, but a certainty.

Signing a publishing contract is certainly something to celebrate, as it always has been, but it's no guarantee of success. Publishers make mistakes, just like the rest of us, pulping the 'next big thing' when it fails to find an audience, and passing up the chance to publish a blockbuster without ever seeing its brilliance.

'For hundreds of years, writers couldn't reach readers without publishers. We needed them. Now, suddenly, we don't. But publishers don't seem to be taking this Very Important Fact into account.'

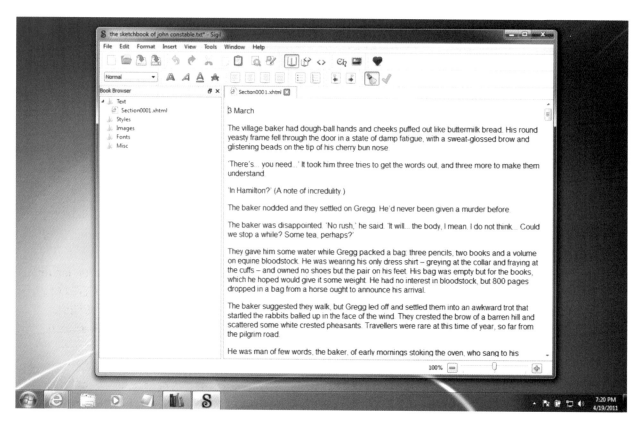

Above: Importing your raw text into Sigil is the first step in converting your document into a properly organised, sellable Kindle book.

The publishing world it littered with stories of successful stories who were turned down time and time again when they were just starting out and trying to get overworked, time-short publishers to show some interest in their work. JK Rowling and Stephen King, both household names with millions of book sales behind them, went through the process of sending samples of their work to leading agents and publishing houses, only to receive a rejection slip in return.

Remember, though, that success comes through actually selling books, not simply through having a Penguin embossed on your cover. So, the more you sell, the greater your success, but how do you sell without a publisher? It isn't easy in print. The biggest sellers in any bookshop are stacked on the tables inside the door. Without a spot on the table, your chance of success is greatly diminished, but landing one is expensive.

That's where publishers are of greatest help to the first-time author. Bookshops can't afford to take a risk any more than a publisher can, and so often they will only stack books on these tables that have been heavily

promoted in the press and already proved themselves to be likely sellers, either because they have been written by well-known and successful names, or because the publisher has committed a significant budget to promoting the title. Without a publisher you won't be able to afford to compete with them, and so the shop front table is almost certainly out of your reach. So, too, are the readers those tables attract.

There are no tables with eBooks. Publish on Kindle and you'll be given the same virtual shelf space as Dan Brown, and probably earn better royalties. Most mainstream authors receive considerably less than 15% of the cover price for each book sold, but you'll earn up to 70% without any ongoing costs.

You'll also receive your payments sooner. Each of your sales is electronic, so it can be accurately registered right away. Although readers who buy a Kindle book by accident can return it for a refund if they haven't started reading it, the majority of your sales should progress to completion. Amazon will record the royalty against your account and, a few weeks later, you'll receive a cheque or bank transfer, in exchange for your sales.

Compare that to the world of traditional publishing. It can easily take a year or more for a printed book to find an agent, several months for the agent to sell it, and a year to a year and a half for your publisher to edit, print and market it in line with their leisurely schedules. Your royalties will likely be paid every six to 12 months, so your chance of earning anything within three years of typing The End are very slim indeed. Can you afford to wait that long when you have other books to write?

Save yourself the frustration, sidestep the traditional publishing route as we'll show you here, and you can be selling your book

BEYOND KINDLE

Amazon is the most accessible market for first-time authors, but it's far from the only one. Apple's iBookstore signed up 2,500 publishers in its first nine months and sold over 100 million books. Waterstones in the UK sells ebooks for the Sony Reader and in the US Barnes & Noble has its own Nook device. Beyond these there are countless independent outlets targeting third-party devices.

Unless you've registered with the US tax system, the easiest way to sell through each of them is to use an approved aggregator such as *lulu.com*. As well as publishing single-copy print editions of user-uploaded books, Lulu will push content into the iBookstore and other ebook outlets by assigning your novel a free ISBN (International Standard Book Number).

This is a stock control code that uniquely identifies every published book to simplify the cataloguing and ordering process. The numbers are assigned in batches to registered publishers by national agencies of the International Standard Book Numbering Convention. The UK agency is Nielsen Book (*isbn.nielsenbook.co.uk*).

To publish books under your own imprint through Lulu you must register with your local ISBN agency and buy a batch of numbers. In the UK it costs £118.68 (inc VAT) for your first 10 ISBNs. Each subsequent batch of 10 cost £66.36, with discounts open to more prolific publishers. Each ISBN can be used only once, and on one format, so you can't share one between ePub and Kindle versions.

by next weekend. You'll have a three-year head start on your print-based rivals in which to start writing a sequel and beyond.

Formatting your first book for Kindle

In the steps that follow we'll be using Sigil to format our book. Free to download from *code.google. com/p/sigil*, it's a cross-platform ebook editor that uses epub as its native format. They are other platform-specific options, such as

the excellent Scrivener on the Mac (at the time of writing Scrivener for Windows lacks e-book export options) but the following steps should work on Macs and PCs.

Here we'll be working through the formatting of a genuine published Kindle book, *The Sketchbook of John, Constable*. If you'd like to follow along with a copy of the finished book in front of you, download a copy from Amazon UK at *http://amzn. to/gf7fFw* or from the US store at *http://amzn.to/u475sY*.

If your book is a plain text file then you have a head start, as you can open it directly inside Sigil. However, if you wrote it using Word, you'll need to convert it first. From Word, pick *File | Save As...* and choose '*Web Page, Filtered*' as the format. Open the result in Sigil (*see the grab the previous pages*).

Just like web pages, ePub files are highly structured, with their contents described in underlying code and arranged in a particular order so that whatever e-reader they are opened in will know exactly how to render their contents. Most e-readers, including the iBooks software that is free to download for use on the iPad, iPhone and iPod touch, use the ePub format, and although Amazon hinted that it may also allow this format in addition to its native book format in the latest release of its devices, that never happened. What we must do, therefore, is create Kindle-specific books if we want to sell them through its online store.

Right: Import your chosen image and then use the Add Semantics option on the formatting fly-out menu to mark it as your cover.

Our first job is to add the cover. Position your cursor at the very start of the text and press *ctrl-shift-i* (*command-shift-i* on the Mac) to open the image browser. Choose the picture you want to use and it will be added to the Images folder in the Sigil sidebar. At the moment it's nothing more than a floating asset in your raw ePub file and won't ever appear in the finished book until you tell

the e-reader how to use it. We do this using 'semantics', which as the name suggests is merely a signpost describing what the image is and how it should be used, just as we'll later go on to define different text types.

To mark out this image as the cover, then, right click its entry in the sidebar (command-click on the Mac) and choose *Add Semantics | Cover Image* (*see the grab below*).

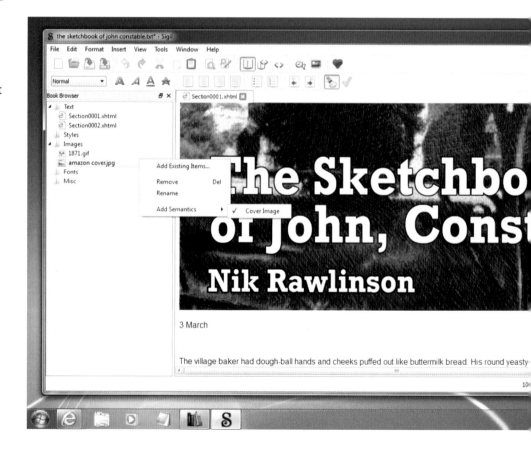

Images that you want to embed within the text are imported in exactly the same way, but without being marked for use as the cover. In *The Sketchbook of John, Constable*, we're using a graphic timeline at the start of each chapter that would be impossible to render accurately using text. You can see what this looks like in the image to the right. Although it looks large, the Kindle will automatically re size it to fit within the bounds of the screen when in the finished book.

At this early stage, your book is a fairly unmanageable tract – Just a long stretch of unformatted text – that needs to be split into chapters. Position your cursor at the very start of chapter one, immediately after the cover image, and press *ctrl-return* (*command-return* on the Mac) to insert a chapter break. Do the same at the

Work your way through your book, inserting breaks within the text to denote the start of each chapter. Each one will appear as a notch on the Kindle progress bar.

start of chapter two. You will now have three files in the sidebar's Text folder with consecutive numbers. *Section0001.xhtml* is your cover, *Section0002.xhtml* is chapter one and *Section0003.xhtml* is the rest of your book, which still needs to be further broken down. Continue working through the text, inserting a break before each chapter to create new files in the sidebar until you come to the end of the text (*see above*).

If you want to include a table of contents in your book, use the style menu on the left of the toolbar as you create your chapters to mark each title as a Heading.

Use the table of contents editor to uncheck any sections that you don't want to appear in the index at the start of your book.

There are six heading styles to choose from, with *Heading 1* uppermost in the hierarchy. Press F7 to open the table of contents editor and uncheck any headings that you don't want to include in the table when you compile your book (*see below*).

Your book is progressing well. You have split up your text into chapter sections and given each one a title so that it's easy to identify on the screen and can be navigated either by clicking the headings in the table of contents, or by using the Kindle's four-way rocker button, clicking left or right to jump backwards or forwards through the novel. You now need to think about how your book is going to be filed and sold online by adding all of the necessary author and title data that will identify it.

Do this by pressing F8 to open the metadata editor and entering at the very least the title of your book and the author's name so that it can be accurately

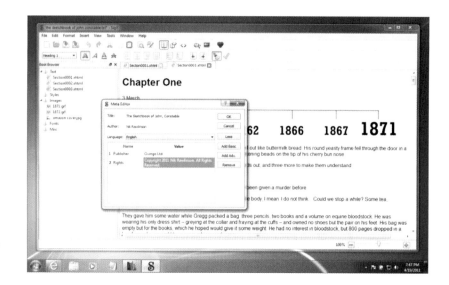

Right: Add at least a book title and author, plus whatever other metadata you feel is appropriate to help identify your book.

catalogued by online stores. To add further details like the imprint, ISBN, rights and so on, click More and use the Add Basic and Add Adv. buttons to add both common and more esoteric metadata. The more you add, the more accurately your book will be catalogued (*see right*).

When you've finished formatting your book, save it in Sigil's native ePub format. This is the format used by the majority of ebook readers, including iBooks on the iPad and iPhone, but not Kindle or Kindle apps, which use a modified version of Mobipocket. While the Kindle Direct Publishing process (*see Publish and Be Damned*) will handle the conversion, for the best and most predictable results you should perform the conversion yourself and test your book locally on your own Kindle wherever possible.

We'll do this using Calibre, an open source ebook library tool that's free to download from *calibre-ebook.com*. When you

first install it you'll have to tell it where to file your library, but beyond that all management tasks, including conversions between different book formats, are conducted through the graphical user interface.

You can add whole books or references to them to your Calibre library in a number of ways, from the simple step of entering an ISBN (*see the Beyond Kindle boxed text*) for which it will retrieve the cover art and metadata, to importing a complete book file for reading and manipulation. We need the latter, so click Add Books and navigate to your formatted epub document (*see above*).

Calibre copies the book to its library and uses the metadata you entered in Sigil to catalogue it.

To check that it has accurately imported your book, double-click its cover in the library to preview the contents. You should be able to click to the start of each chapter in the table of contents, and click forwards and back through the

pages using the purple arrows. If it works as you expect, you're ready to convert it to Kindle's native format.

Click *Convert Books*, and select Mobi as the output format from the pull-down menu at the top right of the conversion panel. The input format should already be set to ePub, our book's current format.

Click *Page Setup* to check that Generic e-ink is selected as the output profile (e-ink is the screen technology used in most Kindle models). If it is, click *OK* to perform the conversion. From here on everything is automated. The progress spinner at the bottom of the library window will show you it's working, but when it stops it won't be immediately obvious where it's put the completed document. To find it, select the book in the library and click the link beside Path in the book details pane.

Connect your Kindle to a free USB port and either drag the Mobipocket-formatted book to its

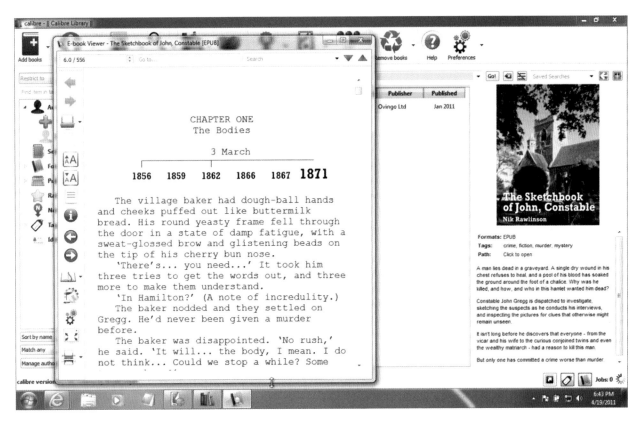

Documents folder, or use the Send to device button on the Calibre toolbar to upload it. You can then eject your Kindle in the usual way.

Your new book will appear at the top of the Kindle home screen. Open it in the usual way to check that it looks like you expected and that you're happy for it to be published on Amazon in this form. Check in particular that the table of contents is in tact (press *Menu | Go to... | table of contents*) and that clicking the links there takes you to the relevant points in the book. Check also that your chapter markers are in place. These are the notches cut into the progress bar at the foot of the reading display. Using the left- and right-hand edges of the four-way controller skips you backwards and

forwards a chapter at a time, rather than moving page by page. (*see grab, above*).

If it all works as you expected, you're ready to take the final step and publish your book on Amazon.

Publish and be damned

Log in to the Kindle Direct Publishing dashboard at *http://kdp. amazon.com* using your regular Amazon account details. Before you can sell books through the online store you'll need to agree to Amazon's terms and conditions. You will also see a warning in the top corner of the Dashboard screens warning you that your account information is incomplete. Click it and enter your address and how you'd like to be paid. You'll

Above: The Calibre ebook processing and management tool makes short work of converting your ePub-formatted publication into the Mobipocket format used by Amazon's Kindle products, apps and browser-based readers.

have to wait until you hit £100 of sales if you want to be paid by cheque, but if you're happy to accept an electronic funds transfer (EFT) straight into your bank account, Amazon will make a payment for every £10 earned. You'll need to choose cheque or EFT for each of the territories in which Amazon sells electronic books, but bear in mind that foreign sales will be paid into your account in that country's local currency, for which your bank

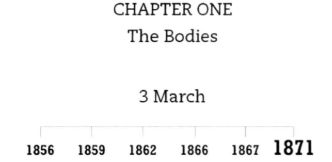

CHAPTER ONE
The Bodies

3 March

1856   1859   1862   1866   1867   **1871**

The village baker had dough-ball hands and cheeks puffed out like buttermilk bread. His round yeasty frame fell through the door in a state of damp fatigue, with a sweat-glossed brow and glistening beads on the tip of his cherry bun nose.

'There's... you need...' It took him three tries to get the words out, and three more to make them understand.

'In Hamilton?' (A note of incredulity.)

1%

Left: After conversion to Mobipocket format our book is compatible with the Kindle. Copying it to our device lets us check that it looks like we want and that the contents, navigation and chapter headings work properly.

may charge a handling fee. Once you have agreed to the terms and conditions and entered your address and account details you can start the publishing process.

Return to your bookshelf and click *Add a new title*. Work your way through the publishing form, at the very least giving a title, language and author name, as well as a description of up to 4,000 characters. This is the blurb that appears on the book's listings page, both on the Amazon web pages and the store pages accessed directly through the Kindle, so think carefully about what you write here and come up with something that showcases your work.

Amazon needs to know where to file your book in its catalogue by specifying the categories under which it should be filed. You'll need to select the two most relevant options, and at the same time can optionally type in your own descriptive tags to help improve its search performance (*see top right*).

Amazon sells both public domain books and those for which copyright still applies, and requires all publishers to specify into which camp their book falls. Public domain books can still be charged for, even if you haven't contributed to them yourself, but they only ever attract royalties of 35%.

It's up to you whether or not you upload a cover image, but we'd strongly recommend it. If you don't, Amazon will use a flat placeholder that will do little to sell your work. Remember, the key thing to keep in mind when working your way through these screens is that everything you do should help to entice readers and generate more sales – and thus more revenue – for you. A well-designed cover image is a key part of this.

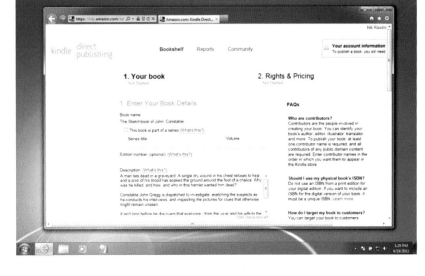

Ensure that whatever image you choose it is RGB, rather than CMYK, at least 500 pixels wide and no more than 1,280 pixels tall. If your background is white, add a 3-pixel thick grey border to help it stand out on the Amazon listing pages. This cover image isn't the same as the one that forms part of your book: that's embedded within the Kindle file itself, so can be optimised for the Kindle screen.

Still with us? Good. You're almost there.

Finally, you need to decide whether you want to enable Digital Rights Management (DRM) and then upload your actual book file.

Digital Rights Management is a way in which your book can be encoded such that it can't be passed on from one reader to another, except in line with Amazon's usual rules about loaning books. You can't change your mind on the DRM issue after publishing so think very carefully whether you're happy for people to share your work without making

Right: Decide how much you want to charge for your book, bearing in mind that this will affect the level of royalties you will receive.

Above: Work your way through the publishing screens to write an enticing description of your book and add metadata to help file it.

any further payments to yourself before going beyond this point.

Amazon will check your uploaded file and, assuming it meets its requirements, will let you complete the publishing process. This involves choosing the territories in which the book should be sold and what royalties you'd like to earn. The standard

share is 35% of the cover price, but if price your book between £1.49 and £6.99 and enable lending you can hike it to a very generous 70% in the UK and US (*see below*).

Think back to what we said earlier here: by following the traditional publishing route you would be lucky to earn royalties of around 15% on net receipts – i.e. wholesale prices, after discounts of 50% or more have been given to retailers as an inducement to take your book. On a £7.99 / $7.99 book, then, even if you swing

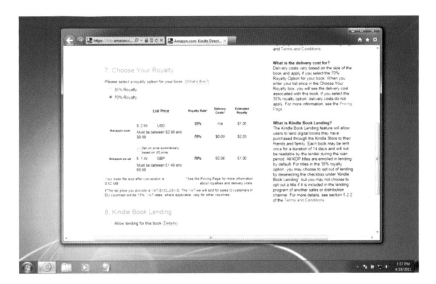

Above: Always test your book on a variety of dedicated hardware devices or Kindle applications.

royalties of 15%, you might earn 59p / 59c. From this, your agent would also take a cut of 10% to 15%.

Sell your book for £1.99 / $1.99 on Kindle, on the other hand, and you can opt for 70% royalties, which will earn you £1.39 / $1.39 per copy while still significantly undercutting the mainstream publishers and increasing your chance of a sale. Reduce your price yet further to the lowest level at which you'd qualify for 70% royalties, and you'd still earn over £1 / $1 for each copy sold, while encouraging readers to buy a copy of your book because it is such a bargain when compared to mainstream novelists' work.

Don't believe us? There's plenty of evidence that it works.

Novelist Joe Konrath was selling his book, The List, for $2.99. Through the first two weeks of February 2011 it sold an average of 43 copies a day, each of which earned him royalties of 70%, pulling in $87 daily. On the 15th of the month, he dropped the price to just 99 cents – a level that is eligible for royalties of only 35% – and sales increased massively. It went from being the 1078th best-selling charged-for book in

the Kindle Store to 78th. Daily sales increased to 533 copies, and although the amount of money earned by each one fell from $2.03 to just 35 cents, his average daily earnings now stood at $187. Dropping the price has more than paid for itself in his case.

UK ebook publishers should bear in mind when setting your pricing that Customs and Excise counts ebooks as 'services' (the service being the act of serving the download), and as services attract VAT this will also apply to your

ebook. Amazon adds this to your asking price using the rate charged in Luxembourg at the time of purchase. At the time of writing this stands at 15%, so if you're looking to hit the magical 99p price point you'll actually have to price your book at just 86p. From this you'll earn 30p per copy. At this price you'll either need to sell a lot of copies to make it worth your while, or be writing and publishing books for fun and satisfaction.

Amazon will 'deliver' your book electronically for free if you opt for 35% royalties, but if you choose 70% it will charge you 10p (UK) or 15 cents (US and Canada) per megabyte to send it to your

readers. The size of the book is calculated when you upload it, and the charge worked out pro-rata to the nearest kilobyte. So, a book that weighs in at 200KB would cost 2p or 3 cents to deliver, depending on territory, which would be deducted from your royalties.

Although words and numbers don't consume a great deal of either storage space or bandwidth when delivered, images are considerably more space-hungry, which is why comparatively few highly illustrative books have traditionally been converted for sale through the Kindle store. This is because they must each be encoded and embedded within the book, and is the reason why the timeline graphics that we used when formatting *The Sketchbook of John, Constable*, were kept very simple are in just one colour.

It is therefore worth thinking very carefully before including purely decorative images in your book – even as markers to appear at the end of a chapter of between sections. Often these can be replaced by regular characters which, however ornate they appear to be, would each only count as a single letter and so dramatically reduce the cost of

delivering your book. Further, it is often better to simply leave a single blank line between sections within a chapter as readers are already familiar with this convention from its widespread use in printed books.

If you do need to include images then you should be sure to use your image editor's save for web function to intelligently compress those you do use and minimise your charges. Careful, judicious use of this tool often allows you to significantly reduce the file size of an image without having any visible detrimental effect on its appearance. This is because the human eye is better at detecting interference in parts of an image demonstrating significant change, and so it can safely reduce the amount of information used to describe the make-up of flatter, simpler areas. Throwing away this redundant data will significantly reduce your delivery bills and increase your overall income.

Above: At the end of our publishing and approval process our book is online and ready for download.

Because of the approval process involved, it usually takes Amazon two working days to publish an English language book, after which the Dashboard's Reports section will show your earnings week by week. It takes longer to publish in foreign languages, so don't leave things until the last moment. If you are planning on publishing to meet a particular deadline, plan ahead and be prepared to have your book on the digital shelves a little earlier than required so that you don't risk missing out on potential sales later on.

Now that you know how our book was produced, you can find our results and download the ebook formatted in this feature from *http://amzn.to/gf7fFw* on the UK Amazon store, and *http://amzn.to/u475sY* from Amazon.com.

Hidden Kindle features

Thought your Kindle was just an ebook reader? Think again. Amazon has built in several hidden features, which are easily uncovered with a little smart web searching.

These tips rely on having a keyboard, so work on most Kindle 2, Kindle DX and Kindle Keyboard models. Some other features, which work across all models, such as the web browser aren't actually hidden despite not taking a main menu position, but are instead deemed 'experimental'.

Kindle picture viewer

Your Kindle may only have a monochrome screen, but that doesn't stop publishers putting images in their books – or, indeed, on their covers. So, why shouldn't you also take advantage of its ability to render a good pictures and use it as a quick and easy way to carry around a few of your own images to enjoy on the move or share with friends?

Transferring them to your device is easy. Start by connecting your Kindle to your PC or Mac and opening its internal storage. Here you should find four folders: *audible*, *documents*, *music* and *pictures*. If any of them are missing you can create them using Windows Explorer or the OS X Finder.

Optimise your pictures for display on the Kindle's monochrome screen to reduce their file sizes. Optionally convert them to greyscale, and if possible reduce the image size so that it is no more than 900 in any direction, vertically or horizontally. Although your Kindle will accept larger images and shrink them down to fit on the screen, you're just wasting space on your device if you force it to do this as it will have to throw away a lot of the excess data in the process.

Now create a folder inside pictures to hold your new images.

We've called ours 'holiday' (*see below*) and dropped our pictures into it.

Eject your Kindle and if the new folder doesn't appear on the Home screen press *Alt* and *Z* to refresh the listing. Select the new folder, which will appear in the list of books, and the first of your photos will load for your gallery.

Use the regular forward and backwards page turning buttons to move through the album, and press the Aa button to change the gallery options (*see right*), choosing whether to show the whole of the image on screen or stretch it to fit the height or width, and whether you want to rotate your Kindle display, which works well with landscape shots.

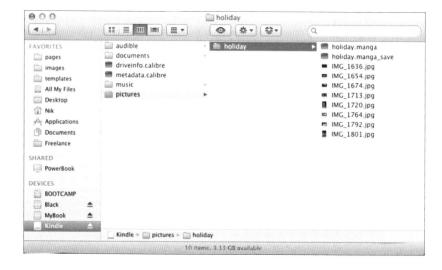

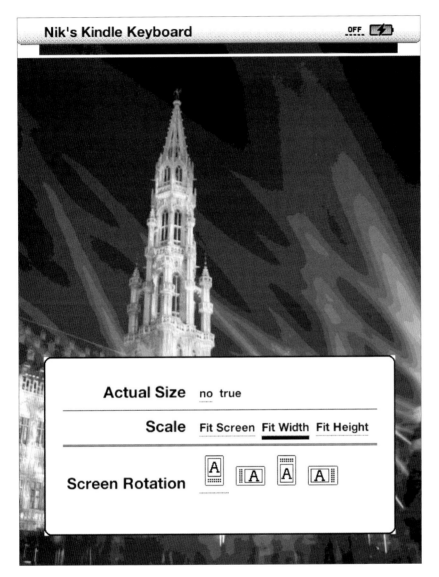

Above and left: The Kindle's built-in image viewing application can access files saved in your Photos folder and display them in a number of different orientations and sizes. If you have a range of images in both portrait and landscape orientation, setting the Scale option to 'Fit Screen' will adjust the each one so that none of it is cut off, although you may have white borders on two sides.

A SHORTCUT FOR TAPPING OUT NUMBERS

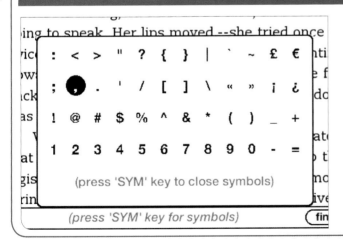

The accepted method of entering numbers is to switch to the *SYM* keyboard and use the four-way controller to hunt and peck the on-screen characters to enter each one (*see left*). This is effective, but time consuming. If you only want to enter numbers and you have a Kindle Keyboard, then you can save time by instead holding the *Alt* button while pressing the top row of letter keys. Q to O give you the numbers 1 to 9, while P will give you a zero. Release *Alt* to return to using regular letters.

Music while you read

Who doesn't like to listen to some music while they read their book? Kindle has this covered.

Connect your Kindle Keyboard to your Mac or PC, open its internal storage using a regular Finder or Windows Explorer window, and drop a selection of MP3 tracks into the *Music* folder (you can create this folder if it doesn't exist).

Safely disconnect your Kindle and choose a book to read. To listen to your music in the background, hold *Alt* while pressing *space*; do the same to stop the music, and press *Alt* and *F* to skip to the next track.

Kindle calculator

The Kindle has a fully-fledged Linux operating system under its hood, which in places pokes out through the reading interface, allowing you to take advantage of some of its core features, including maths functions.

To use your Kindle as a calculator, return to the Home screen (this doesn't work from any of the reading screens) and press any character on the keyboard to bring up the search box. Delete that character and replace it with your sum (see our Quick Tip on the previous page for a shortcut for entering numbers). When you have finished tapping in your sum, press the centre of the four-way controller to perform the search and see the result (*see below left*).

You can perform some pretty advanced sums in this way, using braces to mark out parts of a sum that should be performed first, with the answer to that part used in the rest of the calculation, and the caret symbol (^) to mark powers. In this respect $100\string^2$ would be equivalent to 100^2.

Kindle for geeks

Your Kindle isn't as dumb as it looks. In reality, it keeps an eye on everything you do and notes it down in a log. For the truly technical who want to see what's been going on in the background, go to the Home screen and type *;debugOn* followed by return.

Now type *;dumpMessages* and again press return. Your Kindle will freeze for a few seconds as it retrieves all of the data, and then drop it into your list of books, ready to be read.

For a full set of debug menu options, type *~help* and press return to call up a panel showing your options, each of which can be typed as above (*see opposite page*).

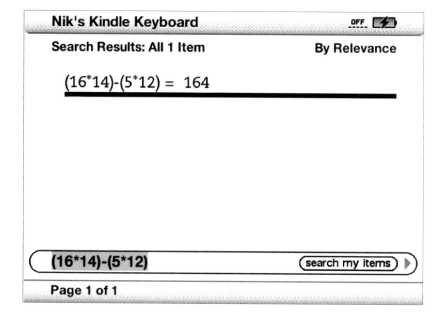

Nik's Kindle Keyboard — OFF

Search Results: All 1 Item — By Relevance

(16*14)-(5*12) = 164

(16*14)-(5*12) — search my items

Page 1 of 1

Text to speech

Too tired to keep reading but want to finish your book? Kindle Keyboard users can press *shift + SYM* to activate its text to speech engine, which will read your book aloud. The results are surprisingly good, and not just for use by bookworms with a visual impairment. Don't forget to plug in headphones if you don't want to disturb those around you on public transport.

Pressing the Aa button when using text to speech opens not the regular font control panel but the

Below: The Kindle operating system includes extensive diagnostics commands.

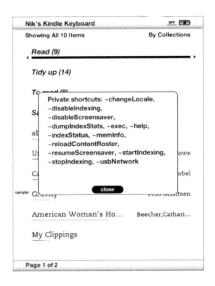

integrated speech controls (*below*), allowing you to change the speed at which the book is read out and whether to use the male or female voice.

In our experience, the male voice seems to give a smoother, less jumpy result, but slowing down the female voice improves it if you prefer her tones.

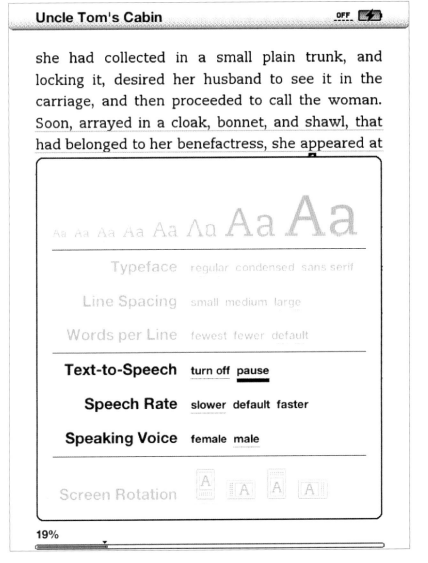

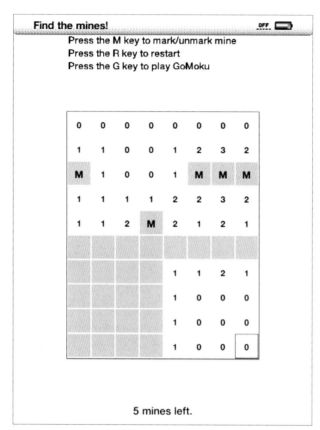

Find the mines!

OFF

Press the M key to mark/unmark mine
Press the R key to restart
Press the G key to play GoMoku

5 mines left.

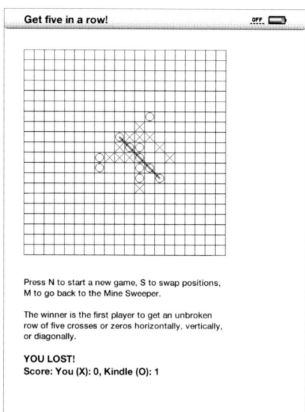

Get five in a row!

OFF

Press N to start a new game, S to swap positions, M to go back to the Mine Sweeper.

The winner is the first player to get an unbroken row of five crosses or zeros horizontally, vertically, or diagonally.

YOU LOST!
Score: You (X): 0, Kindle (O): 1

Kindle Games

If you're buying a Kindle to play games, then invest in a Kindle Fire, which will open up access to the Amazon Appstore from which you can download a wide variety of top games, including Words With Friends and Angry Birds.

If you have a Kindle 2 or Kindle Keyboard, however, and want a quick game or two to pass the time while you're waiting for an appointment, you'll find two hidden in the operating system.

Return to the Home screen and press *Shift-Alt-M* to switch to Mine Sweeper (*above left*).

Windows users will remember this game, but for anyone who hasn't played it, your Kindle has hidden 10 sea mines in an ocean that is eight squares wide and 10 deep. Your task is to find them all without hitting any of them. Use the four-way controller to move your position around the board and press the central button to uncover the highlighted square. Kindle gives you some help by showing how many mines border any particular square to help you avoid a nasty surprise.

If you turn up a square bordered by no mines, Mine Sweeper will reveal a whole block

of empty squares until it reaches a strip that does border a mine.

Once you've mastered Mine Sweeper and try your hand at GoMoku (*above right*). This is like Connect 4 on a grand scale. Your task is to line up five of your 'X' characters in a row, horizontally, vertically or diagonally. Meanwhile, your Kindle will be trying to do the same thing while also blocking you as you get closer to your goal. You therefore need to keep an eye on what it's doing, as if it achieves five in a row before you, you've lost.

To exit the games, press the Home button to return to your list of books.

How to send documents to your Kindle wirelessly

The Kindle is, at heart, a book reader. However, books can come in a wide variety of formats. Most of us think of a traditional book as a bound collection of pages, which in Kindle format has been transformed into a flowing text file with changeable font faces, text sizes and line spacing.

However, the Kindle can also handle a wide range of other document types, including PDF, plain text, Word .doc and .docx, Jpeg, Gif, PNG, BMP and others, so you can read everything from simple characters and numbers to surprisingly complex document layouts, so long as the elements aren't too small to clearly make out on the Kindle screen.

As we have already pointed out, you can load documents onto your Kindle directly by connecting it using the bundled USB cable and dragging them onto the Kindle's internal storage using your Mac or PC's regular filesystem. However, that isn't always the most convenient way to move them from your computer. There will be times when you don't have your USB cable to hand, such as when travelling on holiday, or when you can't physically access the USB

UPLOADED DOCUMENTS AND AMAZON CLOUD

When your document arrives on your Kindle it will be filed under your email address on the Kindle home screen.

At the same time, it will be saved in your account on Amazon's cloud storage servers so that you can access in again in the future using either another Kindle – in particular the Kindle Fire – or a regular computer through a browser or synchronised folder.

Every cloud account comes equipped with 5GB of free cloud storage, which is a generous allocation, but will nonetheless fill up over time – particularly if you email documents to your Kindle for review. If you're getting close to your limit you will therefore need to delete your older documents if you don't want to pay for additional storage. If you don't have a Kindle Fire you can do this through a regular browser.

Log in to your Amazon Cloud account through *amazon.com/clouddrive* and click Documents in the left-hand sidebar. The size of each document is listed beside its name, so you can see which would make the biggest difference if removed from your Drive.

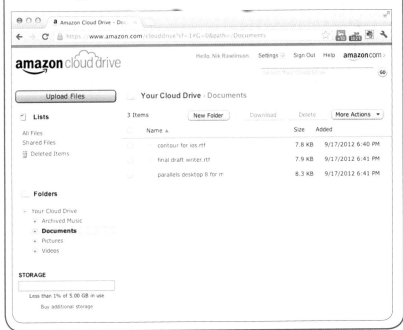

port because you're not using your own computer. On those occasions you'll want to use the second option: wireless transfer.

Transferring files wirelessly

Every Kindle has a wifi connection, and depending on the model you chose to buy, you may also have built-in 3G, which will allow you to download books and documents over the mobile phone network.

Before doing so, you need to authorise your email addresses to send documents to your Kindle. This is an anti-spam measure that Amazon implemented to prevent people from sending random documents to your Kindle device, using up your storage space and Amazon's network bandwidth.

To do this, click *Kindle | Manage Your Kindle | Personal Document Settings* and click the link to *Add a new approved email address*. Double-check before clicking Add Address, and then log out.

QUICK TIP

Document transfers are one-way only operations. You can't transfer documents off your e-ink Kindle by email or any other wireless means, so don't lose your USB cable.

Walkthrough

Skill level	Beginner – a simple task that everyone can complete
Time required	Around five minutes
Equipment	Any Kindle model, including previous versions, plus a computer with a live Internet connection and an email client

STEP BY STEP

1. Start by checking the email address to which you need to send your documents. This will have been set by Amazon and is based on your Amazon account name. Find it by pressing the Kindle menu button and then selecting Settings from the drop-down menu.

2. Navigate to the second page of the settings utility to find your address, which will take the form of *<username>@kindle.com*.

3. If you're not happy with your assigned address you can specify a new one through your Amazon account. Log in using a regular browser and click *Kindle | Manage Your Kindle | Personal Document Settings*. Here you'll find details of the email address assigned to each of your Kindles. To change one of them, click the Edit button at the end of its entry and enter a new username. You can't change the *@kindle.com* part of the address. Very obvious names will already have been taken, so you may have to use a little trial and error to find one that remains available is you have a common name. There is no reason, though, why you should have an address that is in any way associated with any part of your actual name.

4. Start a new email using your regular email or webmail application, addressed to your Kindle's email address, and attach the file you want to convert and read on your device. You'll receive an email confirming the transfer and, if wireless or 3G is active on your device, the document will appear on your home screen automatically.

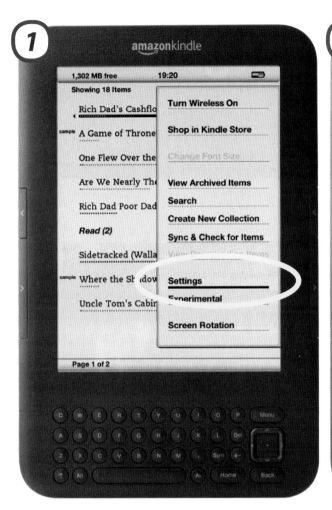

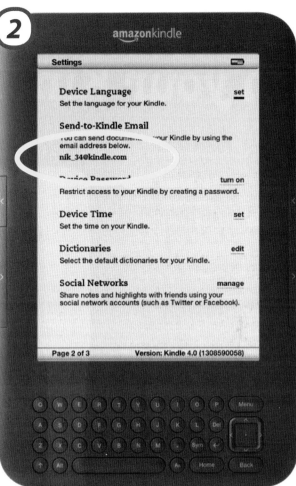

Subscribing to blogs on your Kindle

As well as books, mags and newspapers, your Kindle can subscribe to blogs that will be delivered automatically on a daily basis so that you don't need to check in with each site to see whether it's been updated.

Amazon maintains an extensive list of blogs to which you can subscribe through its Kindle pages. Unfortunately they don't have a direct entry in the Amazon sidebar, so click Kindle and then, from the bar at the top of the screen select Blogs.

Just like books, videos and music, Amazon maintains a list of the most popular blogs. Most of these are charged for, often for around 99p per month on an ongoing subscription, but you can find a handful of free subscriptions from the Top 100 tabbed lists to the right of the page.

To subscribe to a blog, open its full listing and then, in the same way that you would buy a book, select the device to which you want to send the blog updates and click Subscribe with 1-Click (*see grab 1*).

Even if you're subscribing to a free blog, Amazon will want to check that it has valid payment

Subscribing to a blog on your Kindle means you can keep up with your reading in comfort. New bundles of updated articles are sent to your device automatically every day.

details before it will process the subscription. Once you have confirmed these, it will dispatch the first set of compiled stories to your selected Kindle.

Make sure that your Kindle has an active network connection and force it to check for updated content to download the first edition. If you keep your wireless connection active future updates will be pushed down to your device automatically, but keep in mind that doing so will drain your battery more quickly.

Each compiled blog is delivered as a collection of story headlines in a linked index. Clicking an entry in this article list takes you directly to its opening paragraphs.

If you ever decide that you no longer want to receive your blog subscription, don't simply turn off the wireless connection on your Kindle, as any charged related to the subscription will still apply.

Instead, return to the Kindle Dashboard and select Subscription Settings in the sidebar menu. Use the Actions button beside the blog from which you want to unsubscribe to pick *Cancel subscription* (*see right*). This is also the place to order a re-delivery.

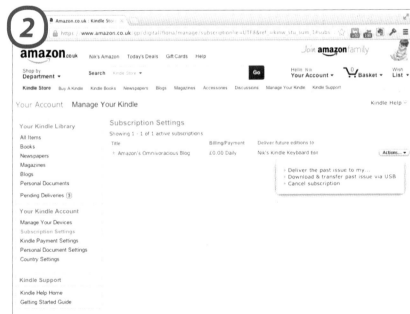

How to manage your Kindle remotely

Although every Kindle has all the tools you need to manage it built in to its operating system, it's often faster – not to mention more convenient – to manage it remotely from any internet-connected PC or Mac.

This allows you to use a full-sized keyboard and mouse, along with your regular browser, to perform what might otherwise be fiddly tasks if you were restricted to using the Kindle's physical or on-screen keyboard and its four way controller.

We have already seen how easy it is to buy books though a regular browser and send them to your Kindle; here we'll take a closer look at the other actions you can perform through the browser using the Kindle dashboard through which Amazon lets you access each of your registered Kindle devices. Get started by picking *Kindle | Manage Your Kindle* from the sidebar. If you haven't recently entered your password you'll need to add it on the next screen to progress any further.

Although you'll spend most of your time reading books on your Kindle, it's also capable of downloading newspapers and magazines and subscribing to blogs, with any daily, weekly or monthly updates published by each one automatically downloaded to your device on a rolling subscription.

You can also, of course, send your own documents to the Kindle, again from the comfort of a regular browser.

Authorising document uploads

One of the simplest ways to get new content onto your Kindle, other than books bought from Amazon, is to email it to the address associated with each device. This is displayed on the top line of its section on the dashboard (*see opposite page*).

Obviously you don't want just anyone sending documents to your device as it would be a target for spammers, so Amazon has put a number of controls in place that keeps it protected.

To prevent your Kindle being spammed, click *Personal Document Settings* and first choose the email addresses at which you want each Kindle to receive incoming documents. Next, scroll down to the *Approved Personal Document E-mail List* section and specify which addresses can send you documents, and add your own day-to-day email address. This will now be the only address that can send documents to your device, effectively locking out anyone else who might try to send it a file.

You can store up to 5GB of documents in your online Kindle library, as well as on your Kindle itself. This feature is turned on by default, but you can disable it by clicking *Edit* in the dashboard's *Personal Document Archiving* section.

Changing your home store

If you bought your Kindle directly from Amazon it will be registered to the national store through which you bought it. This makes it easy to start buying and enjoying content right away. If for any reason you need to change to an alternative national store, perhaps because you've recently moved overseas, click *Country Settings*, followed by the *Learn More* link (clicking the *Change* link at the end of the current country line only lets you update your address).

UK customers can't simply go shopping in the US store (and

NAVIGATE THE KINDLE DASHBOARD

Transfer documents by emailing them to this address. You need a different address for each device.

Use this menu to switch between the different media registered to your account.

Want to sell or give away your Kindle? Be sure to use the Deregister option here to unlink it from your account. You can also deregister Kindle apps using the table below.

Turn of synchronisation if you and a friend are reading the same book, bought on the same account, on different Kindles to prevent one from affecting the other's page position.

vice versa) as though they were tourists. Instead you must transfer your account by clicking *Learn about transferring your Kindle account to Amazon.com* (or *.co.uk*) link and authorising the wholesale device transfer.

This will switch all of your existing purchases to your new chosen Amazon country account and charge you in the new local currency for future purchases. Depending on your bank you may incur currency conversion fees or commission.

How to manage your Kindle library through a browser

1. Log in to your account through your home country's Amazon homepage and select *Kindle | Manage Your Kindle* from the Departments panel on the left hand side of the page. By default this calls up a list of books you've bought on any one of your hardware Kindle devices or Kindle apps installed on a third-party device, such as a tablet, smartphone or iPod touch.

   You can switch to other media types by clicking them in the sidebar, and expand the details of each bought item by clicking the '+' beside its name. Expand the details of one of your books now to start managing your Kindle. Here we've called up the full details of One Flew Over the Cuckoo's Next by Ken Kesey.

2. Click the *View Product Page* link to open the book's original location in Amazon's catalogue, or the *Order Details* link to view full details of your own particular order for that title, including how much you paid, when you bought it and Amazon's order reference. You can also print an order summary here if you bought the book for business purposes and need a receipt or proof of purchase to claim it back on expenses with details of the price that applied at the point of purchase.

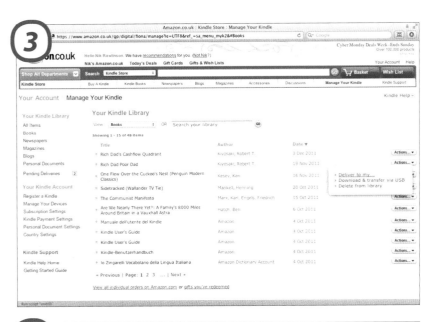

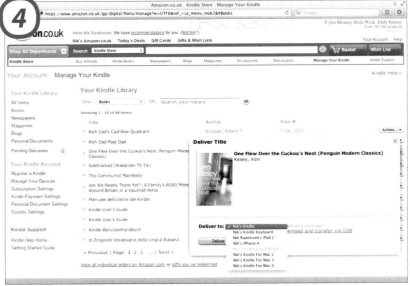

3. Return to the list of products you've downloaded to perform the full set of management tasks. Click the *Actions...* button on the right to call up a menu that allows you to either delete the book from your library or send it to other Kindle devices. Don't delete a book from here without due care, as if you later want to read it again you'll have to purchase a new copy. Deleting a book from your Kindle leaves it in this list so you can download another copy for free.

4. Choose *Deliver to my...* and then select the device you'd like to send it to using Amazon's Whispernet network over either 3G or wifi, depending on your model. All of your hardware Kindles and any registered Kindle apps will already be listed here so all you need to do is choose one.

Note that even if you choose to transfer the book using USB you will still need to specify its destination so that Amazon can apply the necessary Digital Rights Management measures to ensure that the book isn't passed on.

How to set up your Kindle to sync with Instapaper

Now that you know how to send documents to your Kindle you can link it to an Instapaper account to send it documents that you don't have time to read during your regular browsing. Instapaper is a free service that allows you to mark pages for reading later on using a button on your regular desktop, laptop or tablet browser toolbar. Sign up at *instapaper.com*, and drag the toolbar button into your browser (you may need to make the Bookmarks bar visible).

Follow the instructions here to associate your Instapaper and Kindle accounts, and whenever you mark a page you don't have time to read, it'll appear on your Kindle within 24 hours of being saved from your browser.

STEP BY STEP

1. Log in to your Instapaper account using a regular web browser and visit *http://www. instapaper.com/user/kindle* to set up forwarding on your account. Start by checking the box to *Send my Unread articles to my Kindle automatically* and choose from the drop-down boxes whether you'd like them sending daily or weekly (in which case they'll be sent on Friday morning) and how many unread articles there should be in your reading queue to trigger a delivery. We have set ours to 1 new article and daily deliveries so that as soon as we have added a new article that we want to

read it will be delivered to our Kindle within 24 hours. That way it should always be ready for us to pick up on our morning commute.

You now need to authorise Instapaper to load content onto your Kindle. This is a two stage process that takes place half on the Instapaper site and half on your Kindle dashboard. Start by entering your Kindle email address, copying it from your Kindle dashboard to the box on your Instapaper account (it's the address that ends kindle.com). If you're happy to only have documents delivered over wifi select *@free.kindle.com* as the extension. If you have a

①
Instapaper
http://www.instapaper.com/user/kindle

Instapaper   Hello   Extras   Account   Log out

A simple tool to save web pages for reading later.

Manage your Kindle

☑ Send my Unread articles to my Kindle automatically

Send a compilation of up to 20 of my unread articles:

- Every [day ÷] (Weekly deliveries are made on Friday mornings)
- Only if it will contain at least [1 new article ÷] since the last delivery. (reset history)

My Kindle's email address:
nik_34 @ free.kindle.com ÷ See instructions below.

@kindle.com: Works with all Kindle models over 3G and Wi-Fi. Amazon charges fees for delivery. Instapaper assumes no responsibility for charges incurred by your use of this feature.

@free.kindle.com: Works only when online via Wi-Fi.

You'll get confirmation emails from Amazon after every delivery with this option. You can safely ignore and delete them.

If you have an earlier version of the Kindle, you'll receive the emails but the Instapaper documents will not be delivered to your Kindle.

To transfer Kindle files over USB, please use the Kindle feature in the sidebar of the Unread page.

Save changes

Kindle
Fire

Kindle Fire and Kindle Fire HD

Kindle Fire is Amazon's most ambitious reading device to date. With a 7in full colour back-lit LCD display it's a fully-fledged Android-based tablet computer, on which

readers can install their own applications, as well as download books, videos and music from the Amazon online store. For anyone who wants to read magazines just as much as they do books, it's a great choice, allowing them to enjoy pages in rich colour, packed with graphics, original layouts and fonts.

The latest release is the second edition Fire, and the first to be available in the UK. It's been joined by the Fire HD, which has a high resolution display and Dolby stereo sound. In the US, there's also an 8.9in version of the Fire HD, which isn't available in the UK.

Kindle Fire draws on each of Amazon's various businesses and makes their various contents available in your hand. So, not only might you buy your books, music and movies from Amazon, you can

also consume them on a device that's sure to be compatible. Each of these plays a part in making the Fire a success, feeding in up to date info and making it possible to store your own content online.

Amazon Appstore

The Appstore is the place to head when you want to increase your Fire's features. Opened in March 2011, it was the biggest hint of all that Amazon was looking to build its own tablet computer. At the time it had slightly less than 4,000 applications in its catalogue, but this has since grown. It splits revenue with developers on a 70% / 30% basis, with the developers taking the larger proportion and Amazon retaining the rest to cover, among other things, merchant processing and advertising on its digital shelves.

The App Store includes many of the titles that have proved themselves to be big successes on rival platforms, such as Cut the Rope, Angry Birds and Autodesk's SketchBook Mobile. This, perhaps more than anything else apart from its bargain price, makes the Fire the first serious competitor to Apple's market leading iPad.

Amazon Silk

Every Kindle includes a web browser. However, in the case of the regular Kindle, Kindle Paperwhite and Kindle Keyboard, Amazon is very honest about it being an 'experimental' part of the ereader's operating system.

In the Kindle Fire and Fire HD the web browser is an integral and very important part of the way the device works. Although it doesn't include 3G connectivity, the Kindle Fire is designed to be a take anywhere online device that lets you browse the web over wifi without unpacking your bulky notebook computer.

It includes a technology that Amazon has termed Silk, which uses the company's enormous cloud computing server farm to increase the speed at which you can browse the web.

As Amazon explains, a typical web page isn't merely a collection of text and images gathered from one single server. On average, each page you visit calls on around 80 files, which in turn are scattered across up to 13 different domains. These files include photos, text, stylesheets, remotely-hosted fonts and, of course, advertisements.

Many of these resources are actually hosted on Amazon's own servers, while others are hosted elsewhere, on servers with which Amazon's cloud computing infrastructure shares a direct series of fast backbone connections.

Whenever you tap in the address of a page or click a link in the Fire's browser, therefore, it's sent to Amazon's Elastic Compute Cloud servers, which break down the request into smaller parts, working on which bits it would be faster for it to collect itself, and which bits your Fire should go off and find.

By splitting the workload in this way it shortens the time taken to reconstruct the page on your tablet's screen, making the whole thing feel more responsive and allowing you to get more done in less time.

Online content

Manufacturers have quickly come to the realisation that you don't buy a tablet for its specs; you buy it because of what it can do and, more importantly, what it can download. Like the iPad, the Kindle Fire is tied to its manufacturer's own online store, which gives Amazon a head start here. It has spent years building up a varied, yet integrated set of businesses, which together form a virtual shopping mall through which you can buy movie downloads, music and applications.

These are organised on the Kindle Fire's shelves and categorised using the tabs at the top of the screen.

Kindle Fire orientation

Headphone socket

Volume control rocker

Power switch

Screen with resolution of 1024 x 600 (Kindle Fire) or 1280 x 800 (Fire HD)

USB port (also used for charging and data sharing)

HDMI video port

Integrated video camera

Inside: Bluetooth and Wireless Ethernet networking hardware

Twin stereo speakers at rear (with Dolby support on Kindle Fire HD)

Internal storage of 8GB (Kindle Fire) or 16GB / 32GB (Kindle Fire HD)

Tap to return to the home screen

Tap to step back to previous screen

Context-sensitive menu

Search current module

Go to saved favourites

How to get your Kindle Fire online using wifi

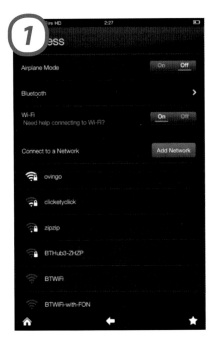

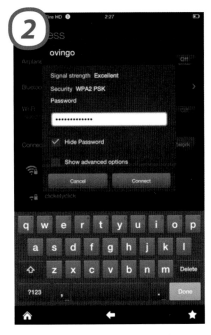

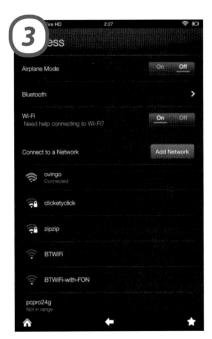

[1] Put your finger on the clock at the top of your Kindle home screen and drag it down. This opens up the general settings screen from which you can access the individual settings zones. This screen also shows you messages, like how many email you have still got to read and whether you are connected to a low powered USB source and thus risk draining the battery.

Tap the Wireless button at the top of the screen to open the wifi settings screens, as seen able. Make sure that Airplane Mode is switched off and Wifi is switched on so you can see your networks.

[2] Your Kindle Fire will list all of the networks that are in range. In our case, that's three networks called 'ovingo', 'clickety click' and 'zipzip' (*see grab 1*). Ovingo gives by far the strongest signal from the Kindle Fire's current position, so that's the one we'll set up as our Internet access point.

Any network with a padlock icon on its wireless strength icon – as is the case for each of these three networks – is protected by a pass key. Your Kindle Fire will automatically select the appropriate security setting for your chosen network and ask for the required password.

[3] Provided you entered the correct password and your network access point is set up to distribute IP addresses on your network, your Kindle will negotiate with the network hardware and connect itself. You can tell that it has successfully connected as the wireless strength indicator turns orange and the padlock is replaced with a tick.

If you ever need to disconnect from your wireless network, simply return to this screen and tap the Off button beside wifi. If you want to switch to another network, tap its name and repeat these three steps.

Setting up your Kindle Fire and Kindle Fire HD

When your Kindle Fire arrives, depending on how and from whom you bought it, you may find that it is little more than a pretty slate. To get the most out of it, you need to hook it up to your Amazon account.

This is a simple process that takes only a couple of seconds, but it relies on you having your Fire already set up to access your wireless network. If you haven't yet done this, follow the instructions on the previous page, and then work your way through the steps on this spread.

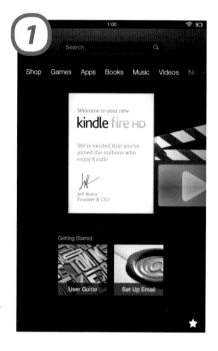

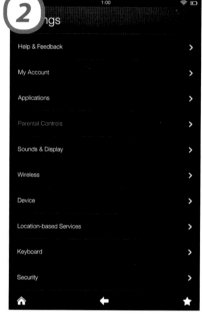

THE FIRE TOOLBAR

The toolbar lets you access the most common Kindle settings, and also calls up an information screen. To access it, place your finger at the top of the screen, on top of the clock, and drag down, then use the buttons to navigate the preferences.

When you first unbox your Kindle, unless it has already been activated by Amazon prior to dispatch it will be in its unregistered, unactivated state. You can still perform limited functions, and access any media that you load onto it by dragging it across using the bundled USB cable, which is also used to charge it (an adaptor plug is an optional extra purchase), but if you want to read your Kindle books, access your Amazon Cloud account, or buy new music, movies and TV content, you'll need to link it to your existing Amazon account.

Put your finger on the clock at the top of the screen in either orientation (we're holding ours upright, but it works just as well in landscape mode) and slide it down the screen. This calls up the Kindle Fire toolbar (see left).

Tap the More icon on the far right of the toolbar to open the complete list of available settings. From here you can manage Parental Controls, wireless networking (see previous page), the way that the keyboard works and – of most interest to us in this instance – your Amazon account. Tap the entry for My Account.

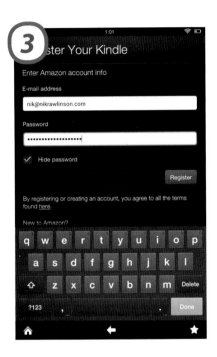

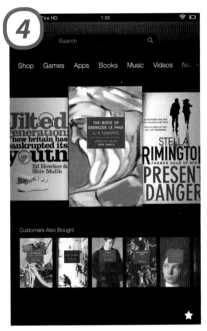

Because your Kindle isn't yet associated with an Amazon account there's not much to see on the screen that follows, except for a Register button. Tap this and the enter the email address and password that you usually use to access your Kindle account through a regular browser.

If you can't remember your password you'll be able to source a reminder from the Amazon site.

Once you have entered your account credentials, tap the Register button to complete the process and send the details over to the Kindle servers.

So long as your Kindle receives a positive response from the servers it accesses your account and downloads the necessary data that allows it to access your purchased media.

Although it has only 16GB or 32GB of storage, your Kindle Fire or Fire HD can access the whole of your back catalogue of content, which you can download to your new device with a single tap.

This brings along with it any supplementary data such as your current position within a book and any highlights and notes you have added.

FIRE STATUS BAR

The status bar that runs across the top of your Kindle Fire home screen and many applications gives you an at-a-glance overview of notifications and status. It saves you hunting around elsewhere on your Kindle for information that is frequently updated throughout the day and between uses that you might otherwise miss. If you can't see it, return to the home screen, as it's always there.

Working from left to right, it shows the name under which your Kindle is registered with Amazon (you can change this through the Kindle dashboard by logging into your account using a regular browser), with the number of notifications to its right. Tapping this opens the notification screen with a summary of your unread email and application notices you might have missed.

Tapping any of the notifications opens the associated application, while tapping *Clear All* empties the list. The USB notification will only disappear when you disconnect your device.

Getting content onto (and off) your Kindle Fire

The ease with which you can get content onto and off your Kindle Fire depends on the kind of content you want to use, and the platforms between which you're moving it.

Moving content on a Windows-based PC

The process of moving content onto and off your Kindle manually is easiest if you're a Windows user.

Simply plug in your Kindle using the supplied USB cable and it will mount on your system like a regular external drive in Windows Explorer. Click it to explore its

contents and to drag content onto and off it (*see grab, below*).

When you have finished managing your files, make sure that you safely eject your Kindle from Windows by right-clicking the USB icon in the system tray and selecting the option to eject the device.

Moving content on a Mac

If you are using a Mac then things are a little more complicated, as the Kindle Fire won't mount directly in the operating system as it did with the previous version Kindle Fire.

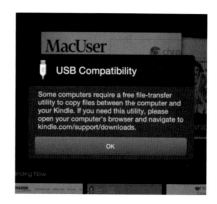

To exchange media files over USB with a Mac it is therefore now necessary to download the Android File Transfer utility, which is free, from *http://www.android.com/filetransfer*. (If you need it on your computer, you'll see the dialogue box *above*.)

This mounts the Kindle Fire in a separate application window, with each of the folders on the device collapsed using disclosure triangles. Click on the triangles to view the contents of each folder, and you can then drag them out to other folders on your Mac in a new Finder window, and drag in files from your Mac in the opposite direction (*see grab, bottom of opposite page*).

You can use this same tool to create new folders on your Kindle by clicking the '+' folder icon on the far right hand end of the toolbar, and delete filed using

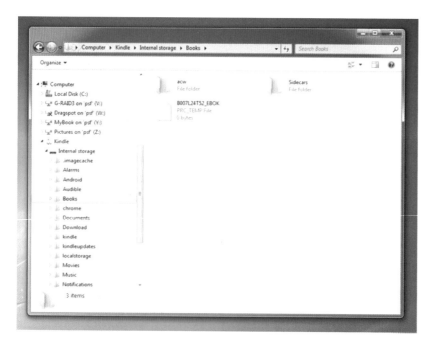

command-backspace in the usual Mac manner, but beware that when you do that the files aren't sent to a trash area from which they can be recovered, but deleted immediately, entirely.

Saving images on the Kindle

There will be times when you want to save images that you come across on the web. You can do this directly on the Kindle Fire and they will be stored in a sub-folder of the Pictures folder.

This is easily done by holding down your finger on the image

you want to save in the Kindle browser and selecting the save option from the menu that pops up after a couple of seconds.

To later access your images, either connect your Kindle to your computer and download them over USB, as explained above, or return to the Kindle home screen and tap Photos on the top level content menu that runs across the top of the screen.

From here, tap the Download album to access all of the images you have saved from the web. Your image downloads will also be referenced on the notifications

screen that appears when you drag down your finger from the clock.

Creating screen grabs

When you want to capture an image of what you can see on your screen, hold down the volume and power buttons simultaneously for a second. The resulting grab will be saved in a Screenshots album in the Photos application.

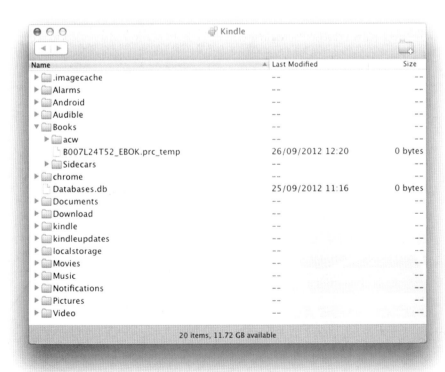

USB STATUS

The whole time your Kindle is connected to your computer, dragging down on the clock will reveal the notifications area, which shows you the status of the connection. In the example below, our Kindle is connected as a media device, meaning it can receive and serve up files, and it's not charging simultaneously because the USB port isn't giving up enough power.

Setting up your email

One of the best things about having a tablet computer like the Kindle Fire and Fire HD is that it allows you to keep in touch with friends, family and business contacts when you're on the move by way of email. Even with just a 7in screen, which is considerably smaller than that on the Apple iPad and Samsung Galaxy Tab, the keyboard remains very useable, and with predictive corrections that let you tap a suggested word as it appears above the keys you can type out long messages in very short order.

The Android-based Kindle Fire operating system therefore includes an email client as one of its pre-installed components, so you don't need to visit the Appstore and hunt through the various options to find the one that best suits your needs.

It has a built-in setup process that walks you through the procedure of adding your own account details, so that within just five minutes, so long as you have all of your login credentials and other data to hand, you can be sending your first message.

All of your applications, including the email client, are installed in the Apps section.

[1] Amazon has built a very large server farm to sit behind the Kindle and Kindle Fire devices that stores all of the content associated with your device. This allows you to keep the bare minimum installed on the device itself so that you don't use up its precious limited storage space. Applications stored on the Cloud can be installed on your device with a single tap.

Open the applications viewer by tapping Apps from the home screen and then tap the Device button. If the email client appears here, tap it to open it. If not, tap the Cloud button, followed by its icon, to download from the server.

[2] As soon as the email client has downloaded and launched, it will recognise that you don't have any accounts set up, and so will open with a view of the new account wizard.

It knows how various accounts should be configured already, which greatly simplifies the process of adding your own. If your account is one of the types listed below, tap it on this screen to move on to the next step. If it isn't, tap Other provider. This is the option you would select if you have an IMAP or POP3 account provided by your ISP that you wanted to use on your Kindle.

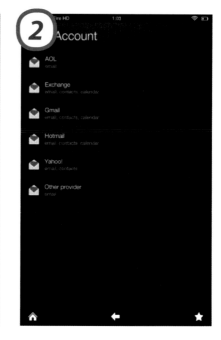

[3] We are setting up a personal domain email address that is hosted on Google's Apps service. This means we've been able to tap the Gmail option and the Kindle has already entered a lot of the details that we need to use to access the service.

If you are setting up anything other than the pre-set account types and run into problems connecting with the server, it's likely to be a security issue. Check with your ISP whether you need to have SSL active when logging in, as a mismatch in this area is one of the most common problems in setting up an email account.

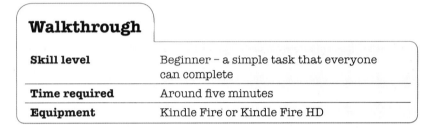

Walkthrough

Skill level	Beginner – a simple task that everyone can complete
Time required	Around five minutes
Equipment	Kindle Fire or Kindle Fire HD

[4] Some account types offer to set up supplementary services, such as synchronising your contacts and calendar with the version you keep on the server. This is a smart move as it means that any data you enter on your Kindle will automatically be synced back to a remote computer, where it will be backed up and from which it can be retrieved should you ever lose your Kindle.

[5] Click Save one final time to complete the process of setting up your email account and you will be immediately taken to the inbox view. As long as you have an active wireless Internet connection it will download the most recent messages from the server.

To send a message, tap the *New* button. Entering a contact name pulls their address from the Contacts application.

Purchasing and organising Kindle Fire applications

The Kindle Fire, Samsung Galaxy Tab, Google Nexus and Apple iPad are the four leading tablet computers for one very good reason: they are both well supported by third-party developers who sell their wares through shops that are tied directly to each tablet's operating system. When Windows 8 is available en masse on similarly-equipped tablet devices we're likely to see a fifth stream of devices added to that list of successes for just the same reason.

The range of applications available for the Kindle is impressive, and in this section we'll show you how to go about buying new apps for your Fire. When you've got them on your device, though, it's important to understand how they are organised.

The Fire home screen is dominated by a large Carousel that organises each of your most recently-used applications, listened to albums, viewed films and read books. They are sorted in reverse order, with the most recent on the left and the others stacked behind it. You can cycle through them by swiping left and right on whichever media appears at the top of the pile, regardless of what it actually is (*see grab, below*). You can manually remove any of these items if you don't want them to appear on your home screen by holding down your finger on their icon and selecting *Remove from Carousel* on the menu that pops up after a few moments.

Although you might quit an application, it is usually still running in the background. If this is causing you problems – perhaps consuming too many system resources – then you can force it to quit fully by opening the notification screen and tapping *More | Applications | Installed Applications*. Tap on the name of the problem application, followed by *Force Stop*.

Favourite applications

Previous versions of the Kindle Fire operating system used to present a series of shelves under the carousel of recently used

Your most recently-used applications and media are arranged in a scrolling stack across the centre of the Kindle Fire home screen, regardless of what they are. Tap an app to re-open it from here.

If an application has stopped responding or you want to free up resources, force it to quit through the installed applications window.

The Appstore presents a wide range of applications, with highlighted choices appearing in a large scrollable carousel at the top of the home screen. What you see on this entry screen is just a subset of the complete catalogue of available applications.

applications and media items on the Fire home screen. These used to display your favourite items so that you could quickly access them, but they've since been removed and replaced with links to content related to whatever is at the top of the stack that you can buy from one of Amazon's online stores.

Favourites are now found in a dedicated menu, which you can access by tapping the star icon in the lower-right corner of the screen. Tapping this calls up an overlay that grows as you add

more applications and media to it.

To add a file or applications to your Favourites area, hold a finger on its icon in the carousel and pick *Add to Favourites* from the menu that pops up (*see right*). Holding down on an icon that is already in your Favourites collection instead calls up the option to remove it.

Deleting applications

Over time you'll find that some of the application you have downloaded from the Appstore are no longer needed, and it

Applications that you use most often should be added to your Favourites from the carousel.

makes sense to delete them so that you can reclaim the space on your device for other uses.

This is done from either the Apps interface (tap *Apps* on the menu strip that runs across the top of the screen) or the carousel. Hold a finger on the application you want to remove and select *Remove from Device* from the menu that pops up. Holding your finger on a media item will instead give you a plain *Delete* option.

Any apps that shipped as part of the Kindle Fire operating system are permanent residents and can't be deleted from the Kindle.

Buying applications

While the Kindle, Kindle Paperwhite and Kindle Keyboard are sealed units that will only ever run the applications installed on them when you first unbox them, the Kindle Fire is a fully-fledged tablet computer, backed up by a well-stocked Appstore.

Although you can view this in a regular browser, if you want to install applications on your Kindle Fire you should instead access it directly from the home screen by tapping *Apps | Store*.

Although the Appstore home screen only displays a list of highlighted applications when you first open it, you can gain access to the complete library either by searching through the box at the top of the screen or using the pop-up menu to access 'All Categories'.

Right: The easiest way to find an application is to use the search box rather than working your way through individual categories. This often brings up related apps alongside the one for which you specifically searched.

Use the search box at the top of the screen to search for particular keywords or application names (*see right*) and, when you find an app you're interested in, tap its name in the listing, to open its full details (*see below*).

Each detailed entry includes a full description of the application, plus screen grabs, reviews and recommendations of other applications that you might like based on this purchase. To download an application, tap its price at the top of the screen (or tap *FREE* if it doesn't have a price). This will change to *Buy App* or *Get App*, depending on whether or not it's charged for.

Tap this new button and the application will be automatically downloaded and installed on your Apps shelves, ready for use.

Note that even if you're downloading a free application you need to have up to date payment details registered with Amazon, so if your credit card has expired or your account doesn't have details tied to it you'll see an error box containing a link that you'll need to tap twice to visit your account and fix the problem.

Buying and renting videos on Kindle Fire

Ask anyone what Amazon does to make its money, and the first thing most people think of is selling books. However, it has for a long time now also sold music and DVDs, and its online movie download and rental service is one of the best on any tablet device.

Movie and TV rights

You can watch any video you buy through its store as many times you want, whenever you want. You can also stream it directly from Amazon by tapping the *Watch Now* button on the video store or from your own online video library. If you're going to be out of reach of an Internet connection

then you can download any video you've bought to your Kindle Fire so that you can watch it on the go without being online. However, make sure you keep track of where your videos are being accessed, as you can only stream them to one device at any one time or download them two devices simultaneously.

Every Kindle Fire comes with one month's free access to Amazon Prime, which as well as offering free delivery on physical products bought from Amazon's store also gives you free access to a wide range of films and TV shows from its online video service.

You can't download any of the films or TV shows to which you have access through Amazon

Prime; you can only stream them. If you want to buy a copy so that you can view it when you're not online and save bandwidth by not having to stream it every time you want to watch it, then you'll have to pay the same price as everyone else.

Buying choices

It's frequently the case that you might buy a DVD and only watch it once or twice. That's not a problem if you've only paid a pound or two to buy it second-hand, but if you bought it brand-new and spent considerably more on it then it can be quite galling.

Although the price of online media sold through Amazon's download store and the equivalent stores maintained by Apple and other retailers is usually cheaper than the physical equivalents on the High Street it still makes sense not to buy a movie if you think you might watch so infrequently.

It therefore pays to explore the rental options available on the video store. Prices vary depending on the quality of the film and its age. A brand-new movie, for example, rents for $3.99 in standard definition and $4.99 in high definition.

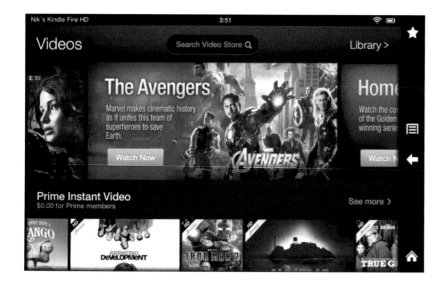

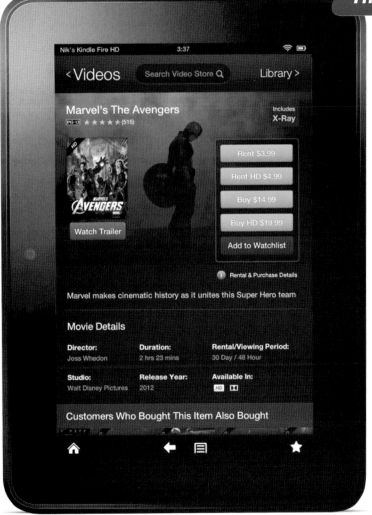

should use when downloading media, press the menu button at the bottom of the store view and select *Settings*. Now use the *HD Download Options* and *SD Download Options* menus (*see below*) to specify whether your Kindle should automatically download the best quality or opt for faster downloads, or whether it should ask for confirmation each time you initiate a new download. From here, you can also clear your video search history, which may be useful if you've been looking up films that you might not want other people to know you've shown an interest in.

When you rent a movie you must start watching it within 30 days of completing the transaction or it will expire whether or not you've pressed play. Once you do start viewing a video that you have rented you must complete it within 48-hours, or again it will expire regardless of whether or not you've reached the end. You can either stream the rental live from the Internet or download it to your device if you're going to be offline at the point you want to watch it. Downloading it doesn't get around the problem of expiration; it will still be unplayable after the deadline.

There are no restrictions on when you must start or complete watching any movie or TV show that you have bought outright.

Quality options

If you're going to be downloading a lot of video then you need to strike a balance between high-quality and low bandwidth.

The former will give you the best viewing experience, but the latter will deliver your movies and TV shows more quickly and with less of an impact on your broadband connection. To specify what settings Kindle Fire

Downloading, organising and playing music

Along with iTunes, Amazon's music download service is one of the most extensive and best-known on the web. It's the perfect partner for the Kindle Fire – particularly since the HD edition now features some of the best speakers you'll find in any tablet device, complete with Dolby decoding.

Buying music

The music player application and the store are linked in to one another. Tap Music in the scrolling top bar on the Fire home page to access your existing tracks, including any stored on your Cloud Player account, and then tap the *Store* link in the top right corner of the interface to enter the shop.

As with the video store, the first thing you'll see is a list of bestsellers, new releases and recommendations. Each part of the home screen can be scrolled left and right to view more content, and each product is accompanied by a price. You can buy directly from this home screen by tapping the price. The price changes to 'BUY', and tapping for a second time downloads the products

to your Kindle Fire and applies a charge to your Amazon account.

That's fine if you tend to only buy the most popular music, but the products that you see here on the homepage are only a subsection of the complete catalogue.

If you're looking for something specific, use the search box at the top of the page or, if you'd rather wander through the store, tap the menu button at the bottom of the screen and select *Browse* from the

pop-up options. The store lets you browse new releases, bestsellers, and genres.

The first two speak for themselves, but the third – genres – opens up a list of different musical styles, including blues, classical, folk, jazz and pop. So long as you know into which category your chosen track, album or artist falls, tapping through these sections is a great way to find other music of a similar style that you might enjoy.

Like the TV and movies store, the MP3 store is home to a far larger catalogue than the home screen might suggest. Be sure to check out the full list of genres to find the track or album you want.

The Amazon MP3 download store offers the same range of tracks through the Kindle Fire implementation as it does through a regular browser.

Downloading tracks

Either search for a specific track, album or artist if you already know what you want, or navigate the genres until you reach a listing.

Tap any album or single to open its full details. Wherever possible, Amazon will display a rating – which is set by other Amazon customers – and, if any have been written, a review.

Reading these ratings and reviews is always helpful when you're researching a new artist, as it will aid you in discovering their best work, but often the best way to make sure that you're going to enjoy listening to what you buy is to audition it, and this is one area in which buying digitally is often a better experience than buying physical media.

Once you've opened an album in the store you'll notice that each track in the listing has a play button to its left. Tapping on one of these plays a 30-second sample of the song. There's no charge to listen to these, as they're designed to help you make sure that it's the track you want and something you'd enjoy.

Auditioning a track as part of an album will automatically start to play the next track once the first comes to an end. You can either leave it running this way until you have auditioned the complete album, or tap the button to the left of whichever track is currently playing to stop the samples.

When you're sure that you want to download an individual track, tap the price on the right-hand side of the screen next to the track name. If you want to buy a complete album, tap the price to the right of the album artwork at the top of the screen. In each instance, the price is swapped out for a BUY button. Tapping this again downloads the track or album and charges your account, just as it does when you buy direct from the store home screen.

You can trial every track in the store by listening to a 30 second sample. To audition an album, press the play button beside the first track and it will cycle through each song until it reaches the end of the listing.

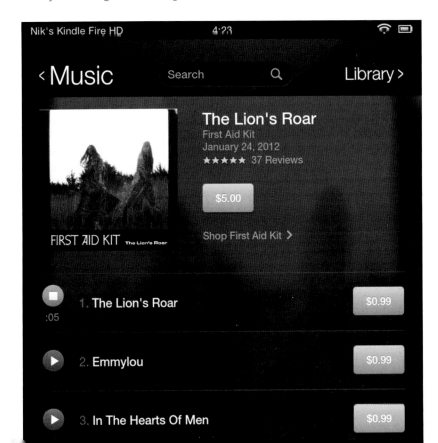

Kindle Fire and Amazon's online Cloud services

Although the Kindle Fire and Kindle Fire HD each already have fairly generous storage built in, it wouldn't be difficult to imagine a day when you managed to fill them up.

DVDs routinely comprise more than 4GB of data, and even if you were to host only a compressed edition of the film itself on your device – not all of the extras that often go with it – you'd probably need at least half a gigabyte free. It wouldn't take many films, albums, photos, incoming email messages, appointments and listings in your address book for you to start running short of space on even the most capacious device.

Fortunately Amazon has a logical answer: move as much of it as possible to the Cloud.

The company has a lot of experience in handling large amounts of data online through its management of one of the world's best-known online stores, which has grown massively beyond its original manifestation. It was only natural, then, that it would lend this knowledge of building online services into its tablet device, too.

Every Amazon account includes access to Cloud Player – its music synchronisation service – and Cloud Drive, which is used to manage documents and other files. You have a fairly generous amount of space on each, with 5GB for your files and 250 slots for music tracks on Cloud Player. If you find either of these is too limited for your needs, though, you can pay to upgrade, with a range of tiered options giving you as much as 1TB of online data storage.

Over the next nine pages, we'll walk you through using both services with Kindle Fire.

STORAGE PRICES

The following fees are payable annually to maintain your Cloud Drive account at each given capacity:

5 GB	.. Free
20 GB	.. $10
50 GB	.. $25
100 GB	.. $50
200 GB	..$100
500 GB	..$250
1000 GB..	..$500

The key content areas in the Kindle Fire operating system give access both to your local device and media stored on the cloud through tabs at the top of the display. Here we are browsing our apps, and downloading the Skype application from the cloud. Once downloaded, it is installed on our Kindle Fire locally so that we don't need to re-download it every time we want to use it in the future.

Use Amazon Cloud Player to synchronise your music

As well as 5GB for your documents and files, Amazon gives you a batch of separate space in your cloud account to store music downloaded using its MP3 store, or uploaded from your computer.

The latter is handled by the free music uploader utility, which is an Adobe Air-based application that works the same way on both the PC and the Mac. The instructions that follow therefore work on both platforms.

Once you have synchronised your music to the Cloud, you can play it through the browser, through a third-party device or on your Kindle Fire and Fire HD, where the tracks appear inside the Music application when you tap on the Cloud tab.

The free Cloud account includes 250 slots for you to fill with your favourite tracks at no cost. If you want to store more than this you'll need to upgrade to the $24.99 annual paid account.

You can access Cloud Player at *amazon.com/cloudplayer* where you'll need to provide your regular Amazon account login credentials to gain entry. You'll also need to authorise your computer and Kindle to synchronise tracks.

Walkthrough

Skill level	Intermediate – you'll need to be happy handling uploads through a browser
Time required	Around 20 minutes
Equipment	Kindle Fire or Kindle Fire HD, a Mac or PC with a music collection, and an active broadband Internet connection

[1] Get started by pointing your browser at the online home of Amazon's Cloud Player at *amazon.com/cloudplayer*. Although we're setting up our account so that we can access our music on our Kindle Fire HD, the whole process starts at the browser end as we need to establish the account and start uploading the first of our tracks.

Unfortunately this isn't something you can do directly through the browser. Instead you need to use Amazon's free importer application, which you can download by clicking the orange button at the centre of the screen. It's an Air application, so if you haven't previously installed Adobe's Air runtime environment it will be downloaded and installed simultaneously alongside the uploader.

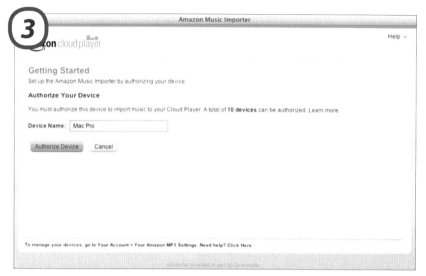

[2] Clicking the link to download the importer gives you full instructions of what the process involves and how to proceed. It's all very self-explanatory.

Once it's installed it will run just like a regular application despite the fact that it's running inside the Adobe Air runtime environment. This is merely a container, like the one used for the BBC iPlayer app, that lets developers create a single application for use across multiple devices without having to recode it for each one.

[3] Although you're setting up your account to share music between your computer and your Kindle, Amazon takes copyright very seriously, just as Apple does with its equivalent service, iTunes Match. For this reason it has limited the number of devices that you can register to your Cloud Player account to just 10. This should be enough to use it on several different computers, through different browsers and on a handful of Kindle devices so that wherever you are, and whatever device you're using, you can still access your synchronised music. Each device needs to be given a name that would allow you to identify it in the future. We'd recommend using a descriptive term for your computer, as we have done here.

[4] Before you can go any further, Amazon will try and upsell you from the free account to a paid-for alternative. You can do this at any point by clicking the upgrade link at the top of the browser-based Cloud Player interface so you can safely take the option to select up to 250 songs for free at this point to see how you get on with the service before you decide whether or not to pay for a commercial account in the future.

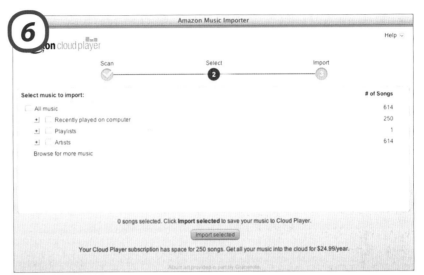

[5] The uploader immediately scans your computer for compatible tracks, checking in your iTunes library and also looking for Windows Media and MP3 files, each of which can be played back on the Kindle (protected AAC tracks downloaded from the iTunes Store can't be played back on Kindle Fire). The amount of time this takes to complete depends on the size of your music collection.

[6] In the previous image, you could see that the uploader had found 615 compatible tracks on our system. This would exceed the limit on our free account so we need to thin them down and choose only the 250 we really want to access remotely. One option is to use these pre-set playlists by checking the boxes beside each one.

[7] However, the playlists are a little inflexible as they were built by the uploader itself. We have therefore clicked the *Browse for more music* option. This opens up a regular file manager window (Windows Explorer on the PC and the Finder on the Mac) through which you can navigate to the folder containing the music you want to upload to Cloud Player. Click Select.

[8] You have one last chance to edit your selection before it's uploaded. If you're sure you're happy with what you've picked, click *Import all* to start the process, making sure that your broadband connection is up and running.

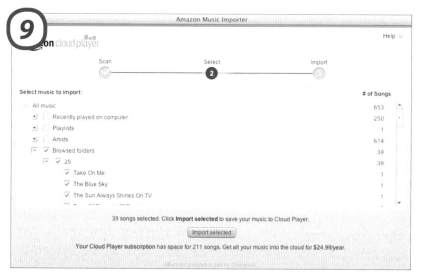

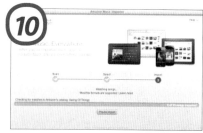

[9] The uploader has added the folder that we selected to the list of playlists. We've expanded it by clicking the '+' button to its left, then opened the album itself, called 25, and selected the tracks that we want to synchronise to our account. We can then click *Import selected* to complete the upload process.

[10] Rather than upload each of your tracks from your computer to the server, Amazon first checks how many of them it sells through its own online store. Any that it finds will be copied to your Cloud Player account directly, both to save time and reduce the amount of data passing over your broadband connection, which help you avoid being liable for any excess useage fees.

[11] You don't need to wait for the uploader to finish sending your files to the server before you start playing them through the browser. Leave the uploader running in the background and return to your browser (if you previously closed it, point it at the Cloud Player site again) and you'll see whichever tracks have already been uploaded in place in the listings window.

Hover over any track name and an icon will appear to the left that, when clicked, starts the song playing. You can also use the transport controls to skip forwards and backwards, and loop or shuffle your tracks.

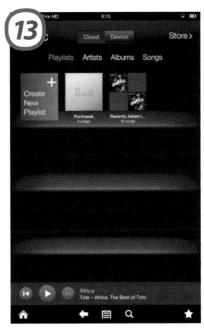

[12] On your Kindle Fire, the same tracks can be accessed through the Cloud tab in the Music application. Again, you need to authorise your Kindle Fire before you can see the music you have uploaded to your Cloud Player account.

Keep in mind that this uses up another of your 10 allocated devices, so even if you've only uploaded some music from your computer and then authorised your Kindle Fire to play it back you've used 20% of your licenses.

Authorisation only takes a few seconds, so if you aren't getting anywhere, make sure your wireless network connection is active and you have a good strong signal to minimise the amount of signal error on the link.

[13] You can organise your music collection into a series of playlists along whichever lines makes most sense to you. At the moment, though, your newly uploaded tracks will be organised in a playlist called *Recently Added to Device*.

Tap this playlist to view the tracks and then decide what you want to do with them. If you want to add them all to your Kindle Fire, tap the *Download all* button to save a copy of each one to your Kindle Fire's local storage.

To download individual tracks, open the playlist with a single tap and then hold your finger on the track you want and select *Download Song*. The same menu lets you buy that artist's other tracks from Amazon.

[14] Tapping a song rather than holding down on it opens it in the Kindle music player. It will take a little while for the track to stream from the servers, and again the exact length of time will depend on the quality of the song and the speed of your network connection.

If, having lived with the limited service for a couple of days, you find that you are happy managing your music this way you might want to upgrade to a paid account so that you don't have to keep removing tracks to maintain some spare capacity in your library.

This is easy to do through the *amazon.com/cloudplayer* website, where you only need click the upgrade link to gain access to a 250,000-track drive.

How to use Amazon Cloud Drive

Cloud Drive is Amazon's online file storage facility. It allows anyone with an Amazon account to keep up to 5GB of files online, which can then be accessed from any web-connected computer – and, of course, the Kindle Fire.

If you have an Amazon account, you already have a Cloud Drive account; to sign in, point a regular desktop or laptop browser at *https://www.amazon.com/ clouddrive* and use your regular Amazon login credentials.

There are two sides to Cloud Drive. On the one hand you have the parts that appear on your Kindle in various applications and in the main content bar; on the other you have a comprehensive web interface.

Amazon allows access to the Cloud Drive from up to eight different devices. However, as it uses cookies to track some of these devices, such as browsers, you may use up one of your allocation by clearing out your cookie cache, so if you use the service with a regular browser be careful to only clear out your cookies selectively, rather than wiping the whole directory.

Visiting your Cloud Drive from different browsers on the same computer will use up more of your Cloud Drive device allocations.

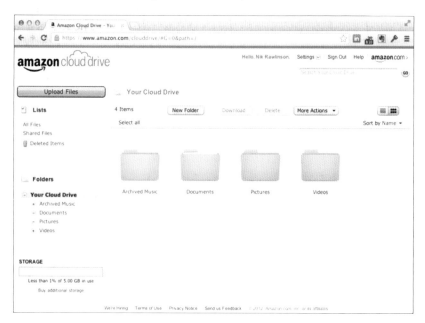

Changing your plan

Although 5GB is a generous amount of space for Amazon to give away for free – particularly considering how many people are eligible for the service – it's still frighteningly easy to fill it quickly in these days of multi-gigabyte video files, office documents and backups.

Amazon therefore makes it easy to buy additional storage, with six tiered plans available to anyone who wants to build on the bundled 5GB.

This option is not currently available in all territories (see the box on the opposite page for a list of excluded countries), but in those where it is available the additional storage will be available immediately.

Unless you cancel the plan or downgrade it at a later date, it will be renewed at your new level at the start of your next billing cycle, so it's important to keep an eye on your anniversary dates to avoid any unexpected bills.

Should you later decide to downgrade your plan the additional storage will remain available until your billing cycle renewal, at which point it will be

COUNTRIES INELIGIBLE FOR DRIVE UPGRADES

- Austria
- Belgium
- Bulgaria
- Cyprus
- Czech Republic
- Denmark
- Estonia
- Finland
- France
- Germany
- Greece
- Hungary
- Ireland
- Italy
- Latvia
- Lithuania
- Luxembourg
- Malta
- Netherlands
- Poland
- Portugal
- Romania
- Slovakia
- Slovenia
- Spain
- Sweden

removed without incurring any additional charge.

Deleting files

When you delete a file, it remains in place but is moved to the trash. It therefore continues to occupy space on your Cloud Drive. You can see how much space it is using by pointing your browser at *https://www.amazon.com/clouddrive/manage/ (see grab, right)*.

To clear out these items and thus increase your available storage space without buying extra capacity, return to your Cloud Drive home page, click *Deleted Items* in the left-hand margin and then click *Permanently Delete All* to remove any files residing in that folder.

Cloud Drive, folders and different file types

Cloud Drive isn't simply a bucket into which you should throw files without some consideration of where to put them. When you first visit the Cloud Drive web interface

(*see grab, opposite page*), you'll notice that it contains four folders – Archived Music, Documents, Photos and Videos. You can add further folders as and when you need them.

By sticking with Amazon's pre-defined folders you'll easily be able to work with your media on your Kindle Fire.

For example, dropping photos into the Pictures folder through your browser will make them appear in the Photos application on your Kindle, from which you can access them to use in other applications or share with friends and family. Further, putting word processed files in the Documents folder will make them available to applications that can access the

The Cloud Drive management pages let you see at a glance how much space you are using and how many tracks you have uploaded to your online Cloud Player.

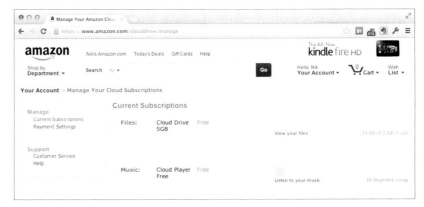

My Documents folder remotely over the net.

Documents

However, it's important note that there is a clear distinction between those documents that you upload manually this way and the ones that you email to your device using the @kindle.com email address specified on your Kindle Dashboard.

Any documents dispatched by email are stored in your Kindle Library. This is different to the Cloud Drive, being the place where Amazon stores a catalogue of books you have previously downloaded to any of your devices or Kindle applications using that account.

Above: By uploading images to the Pictures folder of our Cloud Drive account through a regular web browser, we can then open the Photos application on the Kindle Fire and find them by tapping the Cloud tab. Going on to tap any of the images opens them full screen, or we can use the envelope icon to send them directly using the Kindle's built-in email client.

Below: You can force your Kindle to synchronise its local data with the files stored on Amazon's servers by opening the notifications screen (rest your finger on the clock at the top of the screen and drag down) and tapping the Sync button on the toolbar.

Because your @kindle.com addresses are each tied to a specific device you can send documents straight to the home screen of an e-ink Kindle or the relevant folder on the Kindle Fire.

To find the address of your Kindle Fire without using the browser, open the notification pane and tap More, followed by My Account.

Above: The free Cloud Drive application lets you simply drag and drop files onto an active window to send them to your online storage space.

Below: You can also email documents to the cloud using the Kindle email address assigned to your Fire. Any document with a tick beside its name, as with the first and third in the listing below, has been downloaded to the local Kindle and so will also be found on the Device tab.

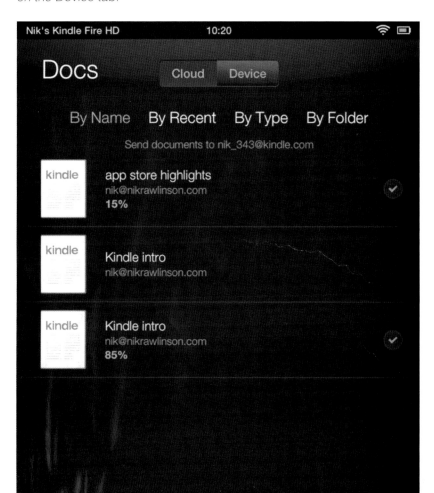

Cloud Drive application

If working through the browser in this way sounds too much like hard work, then don't fret: Amazon has also produced a small application for both Windows and Mac platforms that allows you to upload files directly (*see grab, above*).

This lets you upload complete folders, which transfer from your computer to your online storage space in the background, saving you from keeping a browser window open on your desktop.

On the Mac it adds an Amazon Cloud Drive icon to the menu bar, too, so if you don't even want to open the uploader window you can simply drag files there from the regular file system to start the transfer, and can sync with iPhoto to transfer your photo library.

Files uploaded this way aren't filed into the appropriate folders they way they would be if you dragged them manually through a browser, but are instead sent to a generic Uploads folder.

Working on the move with your Kindle Fire

The Kindle fire is a first-class music and video playback device, web browsing tablet and a gadget to keep in touch with friends and family using the built-in email client. However, if you were to ignore its business potential you would be sorely underselling it.

Built-in business tools

When you first unbox it, you already have access to OfficeSuite, the Kindle Fire's integrated document management tool. It's not a fully fledged office applications suite, but if you find that it does at least half of what you want then you can upgrade through the Appstore to a the complete version, which can also create and edit documents.

As things stand, it can open and display a wide range of common business formats, including Microsoft Word, Excel, Rich Text and plain text. It can duplicate and delete files, and share them with contacts using the built-in email client that comes as part of the Fire operating system.

The suite works in both portrait and landscape orientation, but you will probably find it easiest

OfficeSuite is a free document management tool for the Kindle Fire. Upgrading to the complete version gives you more extensive control over common office documents.

to use when held lengthwise as this most closely resembles what we've come to expect from an office suite through years of using one on a regular computer.

The office suite environment

The hub of OfficeSuite is the file manager. This maintains a list of folders in the left-hand column and the files that they contain in a larger area to the right. You can create new folders to handle your documents by tapping *New* from

the toolbar. This is the only option that appears in this menu in the version installed on your Kindle on arrival. Give the folder a logical name, and click *OK*.

You can't create documents in the same way unless you pay to upgrade, but you can import documents by connecting the Fire to your Mac or PC and dragging them into the Documents folder.

On a Windows-based PC, the Kindle Fire mounts like a regular external storage device. On a Mac, you'll need to download the free

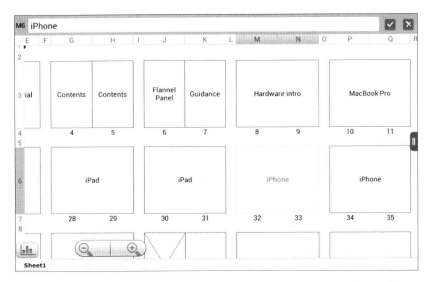

You can easily view Microsoft Word and Excel documents in OfficeSuite, and they render well using the built-in fonts. If you want to edit them, though, you'll have to pay for an upgrade.

Android File Transfer utility from *android.com/filetransfer*.

Once the Kindle Fire is mounted on your system, either natively or through Android File Transfer, navigate to the Documents folder and drag in the files that you want to access. OfficeSuite is compatible with a wide variety of office formats, including the aforementioned Microsoft file types, plus PowerPoint and Acrobat files.

Once you've uploaded your documents, safely eject the Kindle from your computer and return to office suite. If your documents

haven't appeared in the main document window, tap Internal Storage in the sidebar to switch away from the current view, and then tap My Documents again to refresh it. Your newly uploaded files should now be displayed.

Viewing files

Tapping a file opens it in the regular file viewer. The conversion from standard formats is very good in most cases, but if you find that it has trouble rendering a common font that you use in your documents then consider

installing the optional font pack, which extends the range that is installed by default and should help it to render your documents more accurately so that what you see more accurately reflects in their native layouts.

To install the font pack, take OfficeSuite back to the file management screen, tap the menu button and select *Settings | Download font package*. There is a charge for downloading the fonts.

Once you've opened a file you can easily drag its contents around the screen in the usual manner, and if you want to see more of it at once, tap the three dots arranged in a column above the document and select Full Screen to get rid of the menu bar and navigation bar.

You can turn these back on by tapping the tab that sticks in from the right hand edge of the screen, followed by the arrow that returns you to the previous view.

Managing files

If you have a lot of files in your Documents folder it can become difficult to navigate them efficiently. In this instance, use the Filter button on the file

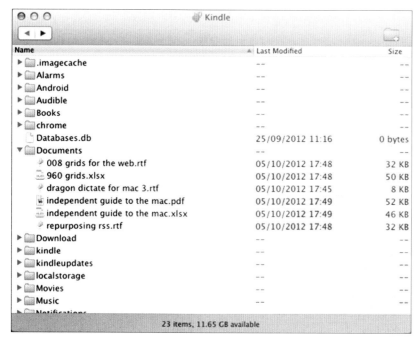

The free Android File Transfer utility allows Mac users to mount the Kindle Fire in the Finder and transfer the documents they want to use in OfficeSuite. Windows users can transfer directly through the Explorer.

the one that comes last in the alphabet appears at the top of the list and vice versa.

Finally, if you have a particularly extensive range of files on your Kindle Fire, you can use the search function to hunt out a specific file name and skip straight to the one you need. Unfortunately, you can't search the content inside your files from this view, so knowing that you wrote about a particular subject but also knowing you didn't use a keyword relevant to it in the filename won't help you identify the document when you search.

management toolbar. This lets you thin out the list of displayed files to only certain types, such as text files, spreadsheets, presentations and so on.

You can also change the order in which your files are displayed using the sort button, which gives you the option of arranging them by name, size, type or the date on which they were last modified.

Selecting the same 'sort' criteria twice in succession sorts the file list in the opposite order. So, the first time you tap *Sort* and *Name* it will organise your file view from A to Z. Repeat the operation and they will be organised so that

If you find that files you have uploaded to the Documents folder don't show up right away, tap Recent files or Internal Storage before returning to My documents to force a refresh.

You can delete files from this interface, but you should only do so with care as they will be removed immediately. Tap the box to the right of the file you want to remove followed by *Delete*, which will now appear on the toolbar. OfficeSuite will ask you to confirm that you want to remove the file and, once you do, it will be deleted from the Fire's internal storage.

Sharing files

Even in this cutdown version, OfficeSuite has all the tools you need to share files with colleagues, and can help to reduce your bandwidth usage by compressing your documents before despatching them.

In a similar way to deleting a file, you start this process by selecting the documents you want to work with by ticking in the boxes to the right-hand side of each one in the list. Select as many as you want to send in one go, followed by *Share* on the toolbar. You can either send the files directly in their native state or compress them by selecting *Zip and send files*. When you do, they'll be attached to an email in the Kindle Fire's native client.

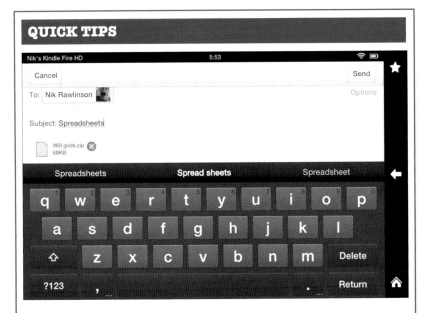

QUICK TIPS

Select several documents at once by ticking the checkboxes to the right of each one, and then use the toolbar at the bottom of the screen to perform multiple operations simultaneously. This allows you, for example, to email documents from one of your online accounts using the Fire's integrated email application without first downloading them and attaching them to a message (*above*). In the same way, you can copy, cut and paste whole documents using the clipboard by selecting their checkboxes and then tapping the appropriate icons on the toolbar. This lets you perform server-side tasks without logging in through the Fire's Silk browser.

To transfer files more quickly and avoid using excess bandwidth on your wireless network, OfficeSuite can compress multiple documents into a single Zip file before dispatching it using the default email client.

Kindle Fixer

Kindle troubleshooter

Registration and hardware issues

I bought my Kindle second hand and it's still registered to the previous user. Help!
You need to deregister the Kindle and tie it to your account instead (although the person who sold it should have done this for you, for their own security).

On an e-ink based Kindle press the menu button and then select *Settings | deregister*. Kindle Fire users, tap *Settings | More | My Account | Deregister*.

If you bought someone a Kindle as a present it will be registered to your account unless you marked it as a gift. You'll need to deregister it yourself before they can start using it. Do this by logging into your Amazon account through the browser and selecting *Kindle | Manage Your Kindle* in the left-hand margin. The next page will display a *Deregister* link beside the gifted Kindle.

You'll now find the Register option in the same position, or follow the instructions on p24 to register the Kindle through your Amazon account in a browser.

I've forgotten my e-ink Kindle's password.
If you've set a password to stop unauthorised users viewing your downloads, it's very important that you don't forget it, as the only way to get back in to your device if you do is to reset the whole thing. As a final resort, switch on your Kindle in the usual way and enter *resetmykindle* in the password box. This will get you back in, but only after deleting all of your content. As this will all be backed up on Amazon's servers you'll be able to download it again from there.

How do I switch off my Kindle?
So long as you've switched off their wifi and 3G features, regular e-ink (i.e. non-Fire) Kindles don't use any more power when in standby than they do when you're reading a page; power is consumed when you turn pages and it has to change the e-ink composition.

However, if you are planning on taking a long journey and want to switch it off entirely while you're away then holding the power switch for 20 seconds will shut it down entirely, blanking the screen so that not even the screensavers show.

My Kindle won't switch on
Most likely this is happening because your battery needs recharging. If your Kindle shipped with a plug, plug it in and leave it to charge overnight. If you don't have a plug, connect it to the USB port of a switched-on computer and again leave it for several hours to top up the battery.

Unplug the Kindle and hold the power switch for several seconds. If it still doesn't work, contact Amazon. Your Kindle is covered by a 12-month limited warranty.

How do I change the name of my Kindle?
Every Kindle registered to your account has its own unique name

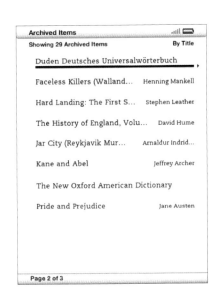

(*left*), which is used in the menu of destination options from which you can choose when sending books to your device.

Amazon picks this name for you when you first register your Kindle, but if it makes more sense for you to use something else, you can change it with ease. Log in to your Amazon account using a regular browser and click *Kindle | Manage My Kindle | Manage Your Devices*. Now click Edit beside the name of the Kindle you want to rename and type in the new details (*see grab, left*).

How do I update my Kindle software?

From time to time Amazon updates the operating system for its Kindles – both current models and legacy devices. These updates patch security issues, improve performance and sometimes add

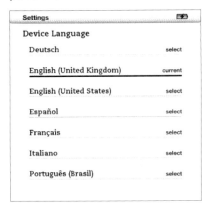

Above: Your existing Kindle content can be easily downloaded to an e-ink or Fire-based Kindle.

new features. You can find the latest updates for your Kindle, including details of how you go about implementing them, at *http://amzn.to/suutAb*.

My Kindle operating system has somehow been set to a foreign language I don't understand. How do I change it back?

The most recent batch of Kindles support German, Spanish, French, Italian, Portuguese and two versions of English (British and American). If you have accidentally changed your language setting on an e-ink Kindle and so don't understand the menus to change it back, press Menu, navigate to the second screen and then choose the first menu option to

pick an alternative (*see left*).

Transferring and syncing content

How do I copy my existing Kindle content to my new Kindle?
There's no need to copy everything over when you buy a new Kindle, as Amazon stores all of your purchases in your library.

To enjoy the same books on your new Kindle as you did on your old one, make sure your wifi connection is active and select *Menu | View Archived Items* to call up a list of your books (*above left*). You can then retrieve any you want on your new device and they'll appear on the Home screen.

On the Kindle Fire, simply open the Books application and tap the Cloud button to view your past purchases. Each one will be accompanied by a down-pointing

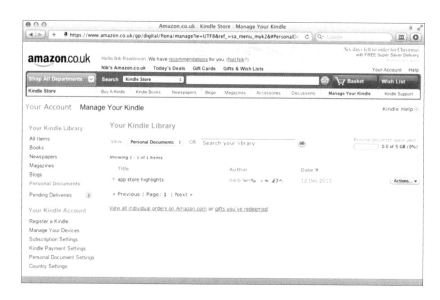

arrow. Tap it to load the book onto your new Kindle.

How to I change my Kindle email address?

This is the address to which you email documents that you want to transfer to your Kindle without dragging them across over USB. Amazon sets one for you when you first register your Kindle, with the extension *@kindle.com*.

To choose a more memorable address, log in to your Amazon account using a regular browser and click *Kindle | Manage My Kindle | Personal Document Settings*.

From this screen, click Edit beside the address of the Kindle for which you want to change the address and enter a new username in front of the @ symbol. You can't change the *kindle.com* part of the address.

While here you should also check the list of authorised addresses allowed to send content to your Kindles to ensure that you have removed any old, out of date entries, and included any address from which you would conceivably send content to your device.

I've emailed a file to my Kindle but it's still not appeared. Where is it?
First, check that your Kindle has

If you're having trouble emailing files to your Kindle, log in to your account and check your Personal Documents folder. If your file doesn't appear there, ask your ISP whether it's experiencing any mail connection problems.

an active network connection and that the address from which you sent the file is authorised to access the device (*see above*). If neither of these is at issue, force it to check for new content by pressing the Menu button and selecting *Sync & Check for Items*.

If this doesn't bring down your file, then you need to make sure that you sent a file type supported by your Kindle. See the box entitled *Supported File Types*, on the facing page, here.

Finally, check the size of your file. Amazon has wisely placed restrictions on the maximum file size that can be transferred to your device in this way. No file can consume more than 50MB of disk space, and you mustn't attach more than 25 documents to a single email, nor address that email to more than 15 different

@kindle.com or *@free.kindle.com* addresses.

Finally, log in to your Amazon account using a regular browser and navigate to *Kindle | Manage Your Kindle | Personal Documents* to see whether your file has even been received at your Kindle address. If not, the problem is likely to be at your local end of the transfer. Check for mail problems with your Internet Service Provider (ISP).

I'm reading the same book on two devices, or a Kindle and a Kindle app, and the pages are out of sync on each device. Why?
Check that both of your devices have an active network connection and can connect to the Internet. They need this to send their current page position, along with any annotations and

FILE TYPES

The Kindle supports the following file types when transferring documents and files by email:

- Word .doc and .docx
- HTML
- Rich Text Format
- Jpeg
- Gif
- PNG
- Bitmap (.bmp)
- PDF
- Kindle format (.azw)
- Mobipocket (.mobi)

When transferring files over USB it enjoys greater file type support, adding the following to those detailed above:

- AAC audio
- AAC+ audio
- Enhanced AAC+ audio
- .3gp audio
- Ogg Vorbis
- Midi
- MP3
- Wave format (.wav)
- H.263 video
- H264 AVC video
- MPEG4
- VP8 video

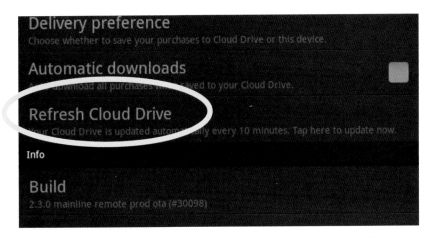

Delivery preference
Choose whether to save your purchases to Cloud Drive or this device.

Automatic downloads
Automatically download all purchases when saved to your Cloud Drive.

Refresh Cloud Drive
Your Cloud Drive is updated automatically every 10 minutes. Tap here to update now.

Info

Build
2.3.0 mainline remote prod ota (#30098)

If your media are failing to show up on your Kindle Fire, it could be that your device isn't seeing the most recent view of the Amazon Cloud. Force it to refresh the view through the music menu.

bookmarks, back to Amazon using Whispersync. In the other direction, they also use it to download any page positions set when reading on companion devices.

If two people are reading the same book bought through the same Amazon account but on different devices, be sure to switch off wifi to avoid each reader interfering with their partner's position in their own copy of the book.

Bear in mind, also, that keeping your wifi or 3G connection active will drain your battery more quickly, so if you are reading your book on only one device it makes sense to keep it switched off unless you specifically need net access.

___

Music

I've bought some MP3s from Amazon and they aren't showing up on my Kindle Fire.
Tracks you have recently purchased can take up to 10 minutes to show up on the Cloud tab of the Music app as they're being synced on the server in the background. You can hurry along the process in a similar way to forcing a Kindle to check for incoming documents by tapping

Music | Menu (the line-filled rectangle at the bottom of the screen) | *Settings | Refresh Cloud Drive* (*see above*).

Note that music streaming isn't available outside of the US, so MP3 downloads won't appear on the Cloud tab for non-US users.

When I connect my Kindle to my computer, I can't see a Music folder in its memory.
Not all Kindles have a music folder by default, but that's not a problem as you can create one yourself using your Mac or PC and from there drag content into it.

However, not all Kindles have music and audio playback features. The entry level Kindle can't play audio as it doesn't have speakers or a headphone socket – even if you bought the non-subsidised version without the special offers. So it doesn't support any audio file types and so creating and populating a music folder would be a waste of storage space.

Glossary

The Kindle may have been designed with ease of use in mind, but it still lives in a world of acronyms and jargon. To really get along with your e-reader, there are a few words and phrases you really ought to know, starting with these.

3G Third-generation mobile phone network technology offering speeds high enough to enable rudimentary video conferencing and mobile television streaming. It is widely available across much of Europe, but was first introduced for public consumption in Japan in 2001. It is used on some regular Kindle devices for buying content.

802.11A/b/g/n Wireless communications standards.

Amazon Silk Browser on the Kindle Fire that splits the work involved in requesting and assembling the various parts of a web page between the tablet device and Amazon's cloud computing network. As much of the content of the pages you view will be cached on the cloud network, as they have also been requested by other users, you should experience a significantly faster browsing experience overall.

Appstore Online shop distributing free and charged-for applications for use on a portable device such as the Kindle Fire, giving users an easy to find, trusted outlet.

Bitrate Means of expressing the number of audio samples processed in a set period of time, usually a second.

Cloud Centralised computing network that is most often used as a virtual storage device. Amazon's specific cloud infrastructure performs two functions: it's a place to store your book, music and video purchases so that they don't always need to be kept on your device, and it's a place where some of the Kindle Fire's processing functions are carried out to take the strain off your tablet device.

Compression When images on a website or music on a Kindle are made smaller so that they either download more quickly or take up less space in the device's memory they are said to have been compressed. Compression involves selectively removing parts of the file that are less easily seen or heard by the human eye and ear and simplifying complex parts.

Digital Rights Management (DRM). Additional encoded data added to a digitised piece of audio or video, or a book, that controls the way in which it will work, usually preventing it from being shared among several users.

e-ink Screen technology used in all Kindles except for the Kindle Fire. Uses reflected light rather than being backlit and so is often easier to read in bright light than an LCD equivalent. Currently monochrome, but colour editions are being developed.

Encoding The process of capturing an analogue data source, such as a sound or an image, and translating it into a digital format. Although files can be encoded with no loss of quality, the process usually also involves compression to reduce file sizes.

Firewall Hardware or software device that controls the flow of data in and out of a machine or network. It can also help to rebuff attacks from hackers. Frequently used by network administrators to ensure that local users do not access external services that could compromise network integrity.

Firmware Software built into a device such as the Kindle that controls all of its core functions. The closest equivalent in a regular computer is the operating system that hosts the various applications it runs. Windows, Linux and Mac OS X are three examples. Amazon has released the source code for the Kindle's operating system so that it can be downloaded and examined by the general public, and also delivers periodic updates that add new features to its devices.

GB Gigabyte. One billion bytes, and a means of measuring the capacity of a device. A byte is made up of eight bits, and a bit is equivalent to a single character, such as a, b, c, 4, 5, 6 and so on. As digital files are encoded using the characters 0 and 1, each digit that makes up part of its encoding will represent one bit, every eight characters will make one byte, every 1,024 bytes will equal a kilobyte and every million kilobytes will equate to a gigabyte (allowing for rounding).

Home Screen As used within this guide, the term used to describe the screen within the various Kindle interfaces that displays the icons for the various installed applications (on Kindle Fire) or the books and other media content that you have downloaded (e-ink-based Kindles).

HTML Acronym for HyperText Mark-up Language, the code used to program web pages. It is a plain-English language code, which uses simple tags such as <b> to denote bold, <i> to instigate italics and <p> to mark the start of a paragraph. Several applications, such as Adobe Dreamweaver, greatly simplify the task of writing web pages by allowing programmers to work in a desktop publishing-style layout mode, rather than having to manipulate raw code. HTML is often supplemented by attached styling information in the form of Cascading Style Sheets (CSS). Browsers combine the two to construct a page.

IMAP Internet Message Access Protocol. A server-based means of hosting incoming and outgoing email messages such that they can be accessed using a remote client such as the email application on the Kindle Fire. The primary benefit of working in this way is that the messages will always be accessible from any device, anywhere and at any time.

Kilobits per second (Kbps) A measurement of the number of audio samples that go to make each second of music in a digitally encoded track. The higher this number, the smoother the sound wave will be, and the truer to the original it will sound.

MP3 Shorthand term used to denote audio tracks encoded using the Motion Picture Expert Group codec 2 (Mpeg-2), level three. Arguably the most common audio format found on the web thanks to its widespread use by portable music players. Capable of being read by most Kindle devices.

OS X Operating system developed by Apple, a variant of which is used inside the iPhone and later versions of the iPod under the name iOS. It allows Kindle users to connect their e-reader using USB, at which point it will appear as though it was a connected hard drive onto which they can drag downloaded content.

Playlist Menu of audio tracks or video files waiting to be played.

Podcast Pre-recorded audio or video programme distributed over the Internet and optimised for playback on portable devices such as the Kindle Fire. Initially considered to be solely of interest to bedroom broadcasters, podcasts have since been embraced by newspaper publishers such as The Guardian and The Times in the UK, as well as international broadcasters like the BBC, which makes much of its spoken content – from both Radio 4 and its popular networks – available in the format.

Pop3 Post Office Protocol 3. This is the predominant technology for email delivery used by most consumer-level Internet service providers. All good email clients, including the one in the Kindle Fire, can use this to receive email.

Push email The technology by which emails are sent from the central server that holds them to a client device, such as a mobile phone or BlackBerry, without the owner having to manually instigate a retrieval for their messages.

Rip A term used to described the act of extracting audio from a CD for digital playback from a computer, or portable device.

SMTP Simple Mail Transfer Protocol. This is the most common – almost default – means of sending email from any client that works on the basis of composing messages using a standalone client rather than web-based.

SSL Secure Sockets Layer. A method used to encrypt data sent across wireless connections and the Internet so that it is less easy for uninvited third parties to intercept and decode .

Sync Short for *sync*hronise. The means of swapping data and purchases between the Kindle and Amazon's network. Traditionally performed using Amazon's Whispersync technology, although you can also transfer content manually by connecting your Kindle to your computer and dragging it across.

USB Universal Serial Bus. A socket, plug and cable system that allows almost any peripheral to be connected to a Mac or PC,

including printers, mice, keyboards and so on. The Kindle also uses USB as a means of exchanging media content with a computer when connected physically and, now that Amazon is not shipping plugs with most of its Kindle products, also a connection through which you can charge your device.

VBR Variable Bit Rate. A means of varying the effective audio resolution of a sound file, such as a song, based on the complexity of its contents.

WAV Short for *WAV*eform audio format. A format used to store audio developed initially by Microsoft and IBM. It remains more popular on Windows computers than Macs and can be played back by some Kindles.

Whispersync Amazon's name for the process of keeping each of the books you are reading updated with your current page, bookmarks, notes and so on,

across multiple devices or Kindle reading applications.

Wi-fi or **Wifi** Once colloquial, but now a generally accepted term for wireless networking. It embodies several standards, of which the four most common are 802.11a, 802.11b, 802.11g and 802.11n. The 'a' and 'g' variants can each achieve a maximum data throughput of 54 megabits per second, while 802.11b runs at 11 megabits per second. 802.11n, the fastest standard at 248 megabits per second, is as yet unratified, although draft standards have allowed it to be built into many wireless devices already, giving it good overall industry support. The Kindle uses 802.11b, g and n for the broad compatibility.

Wireless Access Point Hardware device that connects to your network or broadband connection and replicates the features of wired networks in a wireless form to provide network access to wifi devices such as the Kindle.